Rural Wit & Wisdom

Time-Honored Values from the Heartland

Jerry Apps

Photographs by Steve Apps

FULCRUM
GOLDEN, COLORADO

Text © 2012 Jerry Apps
Photos © 2012 Steve Apps

First published by Amherst Press, 1997
Published by Voyageur Press, 2005
Published by Fulcrum Publishing, 2012

Library of Congress Cataloging-in-Publication Data

Apps, Jerold W., 1934-
  Rural wit and wisdom : time-honored values from the heartland / Jerry Apps ; photos by Steve Apps.
    p. cm.
  Updated and expanded version of: Rural wisdom : time-honored values of the Midwest. Amherst, Wis. : Amherst Press, c1997.
  ISBN 978-1-55591-601-5 (pbk.)
  1. Country life--Middle West--Quotations, maxims, etc. 2. Country life--Middle West--Anecdotes. 3. Middle West--Social life and customs--Quotations, maxims, etc. 4. Middle West--Social life and customs--Anecdotes. 5. Conduct of life--Quotations, maxims, etc. 6. Conduct of life--Anecdotes. I. Apps, Jerold W., 1934- Rural wisdom. II. Title.
  F351.A67 2012
  977--dc23

                                        2012000182

Printed in the United States of America
0 9 8 7 6 5 4 3 2 1

Design by Jack Lenzo

Fulcrum Publishing
4690 Table Mountain Dr., Ste. 100
Golden, CO 80403
800-992-2908 • 303-277-1623
www.fulcrumbooks.com

Contents

Acknowledgments

As is usual for all my books, many people have helped along the way. My wife, Ruth, reads and passes judgment on all of my writing. Everything has to get past her before anyone else sees it. Steve, my photographer son, and I have collaborated on many books. He also reads everything and offers comments. My daughter, Sue, a teacher and author, reads most of my work and offers many useful suggestions for improvement, as does my son Jeff, a businessman with a practical, no-nonsense way of looking at things. And, finally, thanks to Fulcrum Publishing and Sam Scinta for believing in this project and agreeing to bring it out in a new and substantially changed and expanded edition.

Introduction

I began collecting words of wisdom more than fifty years ago when I worked as a county extension agent for the University of Wisconsin's College of Agriculture. I worked in Green Lake and Brown County, Wisconsin, spending two and a half years in each county. My work brought me into daily contact with farmers and other small-town and rural people. As they shared their problems and concerns with me—my job was to help rural people improve their living conditions through the educational programs my office offered—these folks often summed things up with a one-liner of one kind or another, words of wisdom. "Next year will be better," "Isn't that just the way things go?" and so on.

Soon after I began working, I started writing weekly newspaper columns. I ended each column with some words of wisdom. I discovered that not all my educational columns applied to everyone. But folks told me they always read the words of wisdom. Many years later, when I began penning a weekly blog (I continue to do this), I ended each blog entry with "The Old-Timer Says." The Old-Timer shares some of the thousands of words of wisdom I have collected over the years—and again, people read what the Old-Timer has to say often before reading what else is in the blog entry.

My father was a storyteller and a man with many one-liners that seemed to come at just the right moment. These one-liners covered every possible topic from working with animals to describing a pompous politician. You might call these statements a curriculum of knowledge for surviving on a farm, for living a good life, and for getting along in the world.

My parents were farmers their entire lives. They had limited formal education; both attended one-room country schools: my father until grade five, my mother to grade seven. They were both pulled out of school to work before graduating from eighth grade. And work they did, nearly every day of their lives, as they operated a small dairy farm in central Wisconsin, where I was born and grew up. Until the mid-1940s, the home farm had no electricity, and we milked cows by hand twice a day by the light of kerosene barn lanterns. It was a tough life for my mother and father. Besides not having electricity, we had no indoor plumbing, and we heated our drafty farmhouse with wood-burning stoves. My mother cooked and baked on a wood-burning cookstove, ironed clothes with sadirons, and washed clothes with a wringer washing machine powered by a gasoline engine.

As the oldest of three sons in our family (I have twin younger brothers), I worked closely with my dad during my growing-up years, learning the ways of a farmer, developing the skills necessary for animal care, operating machinery properly, making fences, growing a garden, dealing with animal and plant diseases, and, above all, gaining a respect for the land. I listened to the stories and heard the one-liners over and over again as the years passed. While my father was living, the stories were never written down, nor were the words of wisdom ever committed to paper. They were part of the oral history of the family, carried in the heads of those who had heard them and remembered them.

When my father reached ninety years of age and his physical capacities had considerably declined, he reminded me, "Do the best you can with what you've got." He meant it in several ways. Take advantage of your accumulated experience when you face a new situation. And when you are doing something physical, do the best you can with the physical skills and abilities that you have—no matter what your age. And so he did as he continued working, hoeing and digging in his garden until he died at age ninety-three. He was active until six weeks before his death. Those last days of his life he also told me, "Better to wear out than rust out." After he died, I asked the doctor what disease or problem had caused my dad's death.

"No disease. He simply wore out." My dad got his wish.

The day after Dad's death, I wrote across the top of a page in my journal "Things I learned from my father." I thought this might be a good way for me to grieve my loss and that I'd have the list complete in a day or so. Six weeks later, I was still thinking of things I had learned from my father. Much of that material is in this book, along with loads of additional information I've gained from country people over my years of teaching in the field of agriculture.

In addition to the brief words of wisdom, I have listened to and collected stories from country people. The countryside is filled with storytellers, many of them shy and unassuming and generally quiet. But when they get to know you, the stories begin flowing. Most of the stories are true, some of them are partially true, and the occasional story is made up of whole cloth. But they are all stories of the land, stories that come from the minds and hearts of the people who live in the heartland. The stories are of happiness and hard work, hardship and joy. I have learned that as rural people tell their stories, we should remember them, for in these stories are the values and beliefs that have been passed on from generation to generation and make the heartland what it is today. The heartland as I define it includes the rural areas and small towns in twelve states: North and South Dakota; Kansas and Nebraska on the west and Ohio on the east; the northern states of Michigan, Minnesota, and Wisconsin; with Indiana, Illinois, Iowa, and Missouri somewhere in the middle.

The topics in this book range over what people in the heartland have thought and experienced. There is advice about what to wear, what to eat, how to grow a garden, and directions for making sauerkraut. There are comments about the weather, work, and the seasons—especially winter. Family is a theme; so is the family farm. What to do when you get a cold (spread skunk grease on your chest, prepare a whiskey sling, and go to bed early) is here. So is a warning about bathing too often. Additionally, there are guidelines for storytelling and reminders of the importance of stories (stories are the history of a civilization). Finally, there are chapters about savoring the little things, tips for getting along with others, considering when the chores are done, and being one with nature.

Although some of the ideas are rooted in history, many are applicable today. The statements are both serious and light, with some tongue in cheek. Many have meanings that go deeper than the words, just as what you see on the surface of the land is only a sampling of what is really there. Although what you will read here comes from the country, it is my belief, from the reactions I have gotten, that what is here cuts across time and place.

1
Farming

Farmers are the heart and soul of this country. In the settlement years of the heartland, more people worked as farmers than any other occupation. As the years passed, farmers began leaving the land; now, less than 2 percent of the American workforce farms.

The values and beliefs held by farmers who settled the region, and the children and grandchildren who followed them on the land, forged the basic foundation for today's heartland people. Some modern-day folks claim farmers and farm life are historic relics, replaced by high-tech, modern-day agriculturists who farm thousands of acres, milk thousands of cows, fatten thousands of beef cattle in feedlots, and raise thousands of hogs and poultry in confined operations. Those who say this are likely not aware of the much smaller farming operations, many of them organic, that are rapidly growing in number in this country and in many ways resembling the family farmers who worked the soil during pioneer days. Family farmers are a special people. Famed Tuskegee educator Booker T. Washington wrote in 1895, "No race can prosper till it learns there is as much dignity in tilling a field as in writing a poem." That advice still holds.

Here is a sprinkling of farm wisdom:

- A farmer recently won the lottery. When asked what he was going to do with the money, he replied, "I'll keep farming until the money runs out."

- Anyone can farm, but not everyone is a farmer.

- In the business of farming, it's not so important who gets there first as who gets there at all.

- An old horse, an old dog, and an old farmer have much in common: they are slow but wise.

- If you must sing, do it when you're after the cows. Cows don't care if you can't carry a tune.

- Look down when walking in a cow pasture.

- Attention to detail makes all the difference, whether it's plowing a field, building a fence, or teaching a calf to drink out of a pail.

- When cultivating corn with a tractor, keep one eye on the corn row, one eye on the cultivator, one eye looking out for stones, and one eye on the fence at the end of the field.

- Bigger is not better when it comes to farm size. Ability to care for the land ought be a guide, not whether a person can negotiate a loan to buy more.

- Books do not begin to contain what is necessary to become a successful farmer.

- Farmers, more than anyone else, know the meaning of hope and patience—waiting months for a crop with the hope that it will amount to something.

- Farmers produce food and fiber, not products.

Products come from factories. Food and fiber come from the land.

- Farmers seldom have good years, only some years less bad than others.

- Farming is like playing five-card poker with four cards.

- Happiness for a farmer is a barn roof that doesn't leak, a pasture fence that isn't broken, and a daylong rain in May.

- Farming is more than making a living; it is about living and the connection of people to the land.

- Few occupations blend art and science as well as farming—adding a little religion also helps.

- For a farmer, next year will always be better.

- Most farmers know they can make a small fortune in farming, if they start with a large one.

- No machine, no piece of technology can replace the eye of the farmer in caring for animals, producing crops, or appreciating the land.

- Successful farmers know the beliefs and values that made their parents successful, and they try to follow them.

- Successful farming has more to do with values such as hard work, cooperation with neighbors, frugality, caring for the environment, and common sense than with science and technology.

- There is reason to suspect the sanity of a farmer who does not complain.

- Today many farmers produce more to earn less.

- Every year is a good year; some are just better than others.

- The grass may be greener on the other side of the fence, but it doesn't matter if you're not able to climb over.

The Land

Land is essential for farming. It is also the basis for all life on this planet; it is just as important as air, water, and sunshine. On it grow the crops that feed the living creatures of the world. Yet, we too often take the land for granted. We form and re-form it; we dig holes in it, pile it, level it, pour water on it, and drain water from it. We call it dirt when it finds its way into our homes and despise its very existence.

We sometimes attack the land as if it were the enemy—not our friend and ally—not realizing how important it is to the future of all humankind. Farmers know all this. They may not talk about it, but deep within them they know that their livelihoods depend on the land. They know how to listen to the land—most of them, anyway. They listen for its subtle message, for the land is alive with a past, a present, and a future. Farmers and their descendants, and that includes most of us, are people of the land.

- Caring for the land is one of the most important things we can do.

- Destroy a piece of land and you destroy a piece of the future.

- Humankind has been given an allotment of land; what we have is all there is.

- Land is more than an economic asset, for it provides a spiritual dimension to the lives of those who work it and love it.

- No one understands the land as well as farmers, for the land not only supports them but nurtures their souls.

- The history of the land is etched in the faces of the farmers who till it.

- Love the land; it is the foundation for everything.

The Family Farm

When I was a kid, family farms, many of them 80, 120, or 160 acres, were everywhere. A family farm is one on which husband and wife and their children earn a living from the land. They may milk cows, raise hogs, keep sheep, graze beef cattle, sell cash crops—such as potatoes, cucumbers, or green beans—or do some or all of this. They work together as a unit, children and parents, often for long hours, to make sure the animals are cared for and the crops are planted and harvested in a timely manner.

- A family farm is where the entire family works together, plays together, and makes a life together.

- Children growing up on a family farm know where their food comes from and take pride in the fact that they helped produce it.

- Children growing up on a family farm learn the importance of cooperation, of each one pulling a fair share of the workload, and helping each other when necessary.

- Family farm children learn respect: Respect for animals. Respect for the weather. Respect for their elders. And, above all, respect for the land.

- On a family farm, children learn to put the needs of farm animals ahead of their own needs.

- On a family farm, there are chores to be done, animals to be fed, eggs to be gathered, hogs to be tended—daily work that needs doing, without fail. No days off, nor days skipped. A time when children learn responsibility by doing, not by having someone saying it is important.

- The family farm is the model for farming and a model for family—older sharing wisdom with younger, younger sharing enthusiasm with older.

- The kitchen table is often the centerpiece for the family farm, for it is here that the family gathers for three meals a day and shares stories of the present and the past, as well as hopes for the future.

- When a farm is sold, for whatever reason, a part of the family is sold as well. Farmers who live and work the land cannot easily sell and move to the city. Too many emotions are involved and too much history. Usually several generations have grown up and worked the same acreage. To sever a relationship with the land is like losing a child. It is more difficult than words can express.

Milking Cows

On the home farm, for many years we milked cows by hand, every morning, every evening. In those days, we milked fourteen or fifteen cows; my dad milked seven or eight of them, and I milked the rest.

- Cows expect the same fair treatment day after day, no matter how you feel or what has happened to you before you enter the barn. Good advice when working with people as well.

- Learning to know another living creature is never at a higher level than when you are milking a cow.

- Milking cows is a time to warm up after a cold day cutting wood when the temperature is below zero.

- Milking cows is a time for thinking about everything, from what you plan to do when you grow older to the meaning of what you did last night.

- Milking cows teaches patience. Milking can't be hurried much. If you try to speed things up, you'll likely get a wet tail across your face or a big foot planted on your shoe.

- Milking cows with your parents is a wonderful time to discuss those things that take time. There is plenty of time when the cows are milked, time for thoughts to settle in and move around in your mind before they are shared.

- There is no better way to understand an animal than to milk a cow twice a day, every day.

- When milking cows, you learn about individual differences and how they must be attended to. Some cows milk easy, some hard. Some have skittish personalities and jump at the least distraction, such as when a barn cat races in front of them. Others are so docile they wouldn't move if the barn was falling down. Some like to be milked and let you know by lowing softly. A few despise you and let you know it by kicking at you, trying to dump your milk pail, or slapping you in the face with their tails. Yet, in all instances, you make adjustments and keep on milking.

Plowing

- Before the new can be planted, the old must be put aside, plowed under, and buried from view.
- Farmers are never closer to the land than when they are plowing.
- Like the artist who paints a canvas with a brush, a farmer paints the landscape with a plow, creating ribbons of black and brown.
- More so than the calendar, plowing marks the beginning of the farming year, the start of the growing season.
- The smell of newly turned soil is the smell of promise and hope, of crops to come and harvests to gather.
- The worth of a man is measured by how straight a furrow he can plow.

2

Community

It is commonly believed that rural people are loners and prefer living and working by themselves, away from the noise and confusion of urban areas. There is some truth to the statement; many people do live in rural areas because they prefer the country to the city. But they are far from loners; this part of the statement is pure myth. Rural people from the earliest settlement days to the present are models of community, of working together, of sharing and caring for each other. During pioneer days on the farm, families could not have survived without the help of their neighbors. Neighbors worked together, played together, worshipped together, and, yes, grieved together when someone died, a barn burned, or some other calamity visited someone in the community. Farm women came together to make quilts, a practical as well as social activity. Farmers helped each other with the harvest, with sawing wood for the ever-hungry woodstoves that heated farm homes, with pig butchering, and with barn raisings. Whenever a task on the farm required more than a couple people, neighbors gathered to help. Often called bees, these gatherings of neighbors made the work lighter as well as allowed neighbors to know each other better and appreciate each other's differences and similarities.

Rural communities had identities, too. The one-room country school, from the 1840s to the 1960s (a few still operate as schools today, but most are either destroyed or are private homes and museums), often provided the focal point for rural communities and gave the community its name and its identity: Willow Grove, Pine View, Smith, Shady Valley, and many more.

Neighbors

- If you think you have a bucket of problems, try picking up your neighbor's bucket.

- Love thy neighbor, but make sure your fences are in good order.

- Neighbors are always there, even when you don't need them.

- Neighbors stand alone as they stand together.

- No matter how rich we may be, we still need neighbors.

- No matter what their religion, the color of their skin, the songs they sing, or the clothing they wear, those living in your community are your neighbors and must be respected and cared for.

- Nothing is more important than the helping hand of a neighbor.

- Try to do more for your neighbors than they do for you.

- When a neighbor loses, everyone in the neighborhood loses.

- When your neighbor needs help, drop whatever you are doing and help them.

Threshing and Community

When I was a kid, threshing grain was still an important community event, a time when neighbors got together to help each other with the harvest and at the same time enjoy working together. The threshing machine moved from farm to farm in the neighborhood, staying long enough at each place to thresh that neighbor's oats, rye, or wheat. In a neighborhood, the grain mostly ripened at the same time, so when the crop was ready for harvest, farmers hitched their teams of horses to grain binders, cut the grain, and then stood the bundles in shocks to dry for a few days to a week or more—hoping that the weather would remain dry as the grain shocks dried.

Threshing was a social activity. As neighbors worked together, they talked about everything from their crops to the weather and the price of milk and market value of their hogs. When it was mealtime, the work stopped and everyone ate together at the host's house. It was a time of storytelling and laughter. Threshing brought rural people together and gave their community a oneness and an identity.

Much wisdom came from the threshing season, now only a distant memory, as grain combines have replaced threshing machines.

- If it is your job to pitch bundles into the ever-hungry threshing machine and you are becoming tired, toss a few bundles in crosswise. The machine will growl and groan and plug, causing the man in charge to shut down the machine to clean it. You have gained a rest. But be careful; the man in charge knows what you have done, and you are likely to get away with it only once.

- Threshing is that time of year when you can check out all the neighborhood cooks. Some are great, and you try to adjust the threshing progress to make sure that you can eat as many meals at their place as possible. A few are not so great. At these farms, you thresh and leave as quickly as possible, trying to avoid all meals, but usually suffering through at least one.

- When it's time to thresh, it's time to thresh. Nothing is more important. When a neighbor says the threshing machine is coming to the neighborhood, prepare to spend up to a couple weeks helping your neighbors as they will help you when the threshing machine comes to your farm.

- When the day's threshing is done, it is a time to enjoy a bottle of cold beer, usually the favorite brand of the farmer where you are threshing. Everyone had his favorite beer: Berliner, Chief Oshkosh, Point Special, Miller High Life, Blatz, Schlitz, Pabst, Old Style, Leinenkugel, and several others. Great arguments developed over which was the best beer. The arguments, in good fun, went on from farm to farm, but no matter what the label, the beer was always enjoyed at the end of a hot, dusty day.

Local Politicians

Politicians are important people in rural communities. Even though they have long been the brunt of jokes, they are nonetheless prized for helping country people live within the rules and regulations that abound in the countryside as they do everywhere else. Politicians also represent them on matters that go beyond their local communities.

- A successful politician is one who learns how to get along with those with a different perspective and an alternative worldview.

- As the wind blows, so the politician bends.

- Don't expect a politician to do after he is elected what he said he would do while running for office.

- For politicians, and everyone else for that matter, getting along generally means compromise—each side giving a little.

- If you have a beef, a complaint about something the government is doing, voice it. Contact your elected representative. After all, it is your government.

- Many politicians talk and talk, with the hope that they may think of something to say.

- Many a politician's backbone is as stiff as an ice cube in boiling water. In the beginning it is there, but it soon disappears in a puff of steam.

- One-room country school boards were politicians at their best. They knew what they were supposed to do, and they knew who they represented—their neighbors. These local politicians also knew that the decisions they made affected the future of the country, for what is more important than the education of the children?

- People generally deserve who they vote for.

- Politicians depend on the short memories of voters.

- Politics are often too important to be left to the politicians.

- Some of the most important politicians are never elected but still make important contributions to the future direction of their communities.

- Unfortunately, some politicians propose to build bridges where there are no rivers.

- When we blame politicians for their voting record, we should blame ourselves, especially if we failed to vote when they were elected.

3

Work

Work defines rural life, yesterday as well as today. On the farms in the heartland, the workday begins at an early hour, before the sun rises during much of the year, and continues into the evening until the livestock are fed and the evening chores are done.

It is easy to conclude that a rural person's life is one of drudgery. For some it is, but for most the work is enjoyed, nearly all the time, anyway. Some tasks are enjoyed more than others. No one that I knew enjoyed hoeing potatoes or cucumbers hour upon hour under a hot June sun, or forking manure from a calf pen, or walking behind a team of horses pulling a smoothing drag that lifted clouds of dust so thick that you could barely see the horses' heads in front of you.

Other tasks made up for the less desirable ones. Going after the cows on a dewy morning in spring, with birdsong everywhere and the sun edging the horizon, was one of them. Hauling hay into an empty barn, with the sweet smell of drying hay and the satisfaction of seeing the haymows filled to the rafters, was another.

Rural people take great pride in their work. It doesn't matter if the task is picking cucumbers, shocking grain, or making a fence. The job is done well, to the best of the person's ability. Barn builders were a good example of this. When they finished constructing a barn, they brought friends and relatives to see it. For these barn builders, each new barn was a part of who they were, what they believed, and, of course, their craftsmanship.

- A neighbor had two willing hired men. One was willing to work and the other was willing to let him.

- All that you do, do with all your might. Things done by half are never done right.

- An enjoyable job for one person may be another person's torment.

- Better to risk going hungry than to continue on a job you don't like.

- Do you want your tombstone to read, "All he did was work"? How many of us lead our lives as if that were the case?

- Every job can be either pure joy or sheer drudgery—it all depends on your attitude.

- Exchange work with a neighbor, but don't worry about exchanging money. If your neighbor helps you for half a day, expect to help him for half a day. It doesn't matter the task. Don't worry if you believe a half day of chopping wood is worth more than a half day of unloading hay bales. In the end, it will all work out, and you will continue having good neighbors.

- If thoughts of your work consistently awaken you in the dark hours of the night, look for other work.

- If you are not having fun doing something, you won't think much of what you've done.

- It is a joy to work at a job that is worth doing.

- It's not going to get done if you don't start doing it.

- Learn how to work well with others; learn how to work well alone.

- Let your deeds tell your story. Don't blow your horn too loudly, just enough so people won't run over you.

- Many people are more capable than you, and, likewise, many are less capable. Just do your best and don't worry about others.

- No matter how small or how large the task, give it your very best effort.

- No matter how well you believe you are doing your job, there is always someone else who can do it as well or even better.

- On the days when you are unhappy with your job, think of what it would be like without it.

- Recognize that there is good and bad in every

job. The idea is to find work that is more agreeable than disagreeable.

- Some people work so slow you have to set up a stick to see if they are moving.

- Succeeding in work usually means working day after day, year after year, but it also means finding time for fun and family.

- To take work too seriously often takes the fun out of the rest of life.

- Try to do more for others than they do for you.

- Using your head when you work often results in less use of your hands.

- We all can do better than we think we can.

- When you find a job you enjoy doing, you'll never have to work another day in your life.

- When you work for someone else, always do more than what is asked. Come to work earlier than required and stay a little later.

- Who you are is more important than what you have accomplished.

- With a little more effort, what was done well could have been exceptional. We often stop too soon. We are willing to accept "good enough" without striving for something special. When you believe you've done the best job possible, consider this the beginning place for doing something outstanding.

- Work hard, even when no one else is watching.

- Work is never done, so take time to play.

- Work isn't nearly as important as most people would make it.

- Working too hard for too long a time is often harmful. A heavy rain does not continue for an entire day, nor does a deer run without stopping to rest.

- Worrying that your neighbor is achieving more than you prevents you from doing your best.

Getting Things Done

Country people have long ago learned how to work smart—they had to. There was so much to be done that every effort had to count. Some things learned about working smart include the following:

- A task started is half completed. Picking up hay bales in a twenty-acre field is an example. The task looks impossible until the first couple of bales are on the wagon.

- After all is said and done, a lot more will be said than done.

- Asking the right question is two-thirds of the way toward its answer.

- Before acting, it is always wise to ask, "What if I do nothing? Would that be the better choice?"

- Begin each day with the difficult tasks. Thinking about the easier things to come makes the time fly.

- Clear thoughts lead to clear action. Muddled thoughts lead to muddled action.

- Do the work that requires considerable thought when you are fresh.

- Doing work with immediate results, such as splitting wood or painting a fence, helps cushion the times when the work shows little gain, such as when teaching a new calf to drink from a pail or discussing politics with your brother-in-law.

- Don't worry about what you didn't do yesterday; concern yourself with what you will do today.

- If we always waited for inspiration to do something, little would ever be done.

- Inspiration often comes from doing, not the other way around.

- Many know the way; few people walk it.

- Sometimes we must tackle the tasks that we think we cannot do—and be surprised at what we can accomplish.

- The key to getting things done is to know when to leave certain things undone.

- When starting a task, no matter how difficult, work as if it were impossible to fail.

Machines

No question about it, machines have made farm work easier and have taken much of the drudgery out of it. Before the 1850s, farmers did most of their work by hand, from the planting of grain seeds in the spring to harvesting the crop in the fall. With the invention of machines such as the reaper, invented by Cyrus McCormick, and a host of other horse-drawn equipment, farmers' work became a little easier. By the end of World War II, with tractors and electricity coming to almost all farms, farm work was once more transformed, with considerably less manual labor. But the farmers' hours did not diminish, and sometimes, with machines and expanded operations, farmers worked harder than ever. In some cases, farmers became slaves to their machines.

- Be careful that modern machines and technology do not get in the way of intelligent ecology.
- Keep your tools and machinery well-oiled and in good repair. An hour spent oiling and adjusting can prevent three hours of fixing.
- Machines can teach us much if we give them a chance; especially do they teach patience and tolerance.
- Machines do some things well. Humans do some things well. We must be wise enough to know which is which.

- Make sure that you control your machines and that they do not control you.
- Buying a big and expensive machine, no matter if it's a tractor, a corn combine, or a fancy hay baler, doesn't mean more money in your pocket. It often means no money in your pants at all; sometimes you even lose your pants.

Money

The words *money* and *work* often go together—the reason for work is to earn money. That is not always true on the farm. Much of the work does not result in money. Of course, money is necessary to pay taxes, make necessary repairs, and keep everything shipshape around the farm. But farm work can result in other, less tangible benefits as well.

- Money can't buy health, a sunset, a friendship, or a baby's laughter.
- For many of us, time is more valuable than money. You can acquire more money. You cannot acquire more time.

- Friendship cannot be purchased.

- If you don't have the money to buy something, hold off buying until you do. The exception is buying land.

- Even when your income is small, put some money away. You never know when your income will be smaller still or disappear altogether.

- It is no disgrace to be poor, just rather inconvenient at times.

- Living to accumulate money is not living.

- Marry for money and love will come is advice sometimes heard. Unfortunately, those who heed the suggestion usually acquire neither.

- Money and happiness don't agree.

- Never let money come between you and a friend. Better to give a friend some money than to lend it.

- No matter how much money we have accumulated, we all grow old and die.

- One person's wealth is another person's poverty.

- One way to double your money is to fold it over and put it in your pocket.

- Pay your bills on time—a little early, if possible.

- To worry about money is to take your mind away from more important matters.

- Want to feel rich? Count the things you have that money can't buy.

4

When Chores Were Done

Those of us with farm backgrounds know that the chores are never done. There is always one more task to do, a fence to fix, some weeds to hoe, a shed to paint, or a calf pen to clean. Yet, farm people do find time to have fun, to leave the chores behind for a little while and enjoy a few minutes away from the never-ending work that seems to always be a part of farm life.

Go Fishing

Sometimes on a warm summer night when the evening barn chores were done, we'd go fishing, my dad, my two brothers, and I. We fished with cane poles, the kind that were twelve to sixteen feet long and strung with heavy green fishing line a few feet longer than the pole. Pa stored the cane fishing poles that he'd purchased at Hotz's Hardware in Wild Rose under the roof alongside the corncrib. We'd dig earthworms, a few dozen, in a special place back of the chicken house where they were always plentiful. We'd tie the long cane poles over the top of the 1936 Plymouth, securing them to the front and back bumpers of the car with a length of binder twine.

Once at the lake (we had several special ones—Gilbert, Beans, Kusel, Hills, Little Silver), we'd each take our cane pole, unwrap the line, snap on a big red-and-white bobber, and finally thread a long, wiggly worm on a hook. Once we were ready, we flipped the line out into the lake, trying to avoid tangling the line in a tree or bush that usually grew where it shouldn't. At least, that's what my brothers and I thought as we worked to toss our lines onto the smooth surface of the lake. We then waited for the bobber to duck beneath the surface, signaling that we were getting a bite. What kind of fish would take our bait was always a mystery. Sometimes it was a bluegill, other times a bullhead, with its homely head and sharp spines. Sometimes a bass took our bait, or a perch, or even a northern pike. The latter, especially if it weighed three or four pounds or more, resulted in a struggle to land. At such times, Pa would instruct, "Don't try to horse 'em out, grab the line and pull 'em in." And that's what we did, except when we got excited and didn't and broke our cane pole, as a cane pole is not designed for catching anything weighing much more than a pound.

Some fishing wisdom:

- Use the wind direction to predict fishing success:

  - Wind from the west, fish bite the best.

  - Wind from the north and the east, fish bite the least.

  - Wind from the south blows the hook right into the fish's mouth.

- Fishing is always good, catching sometimes not.

- A fish is not caught until it is on shore or in the boat.

- You can't catch a fish if your line isn't in the water.

- Fishing is one of those rare times when it is permissible to exaggerate a bit the results of your efforts.

- No other activity teaches patience as much as does fishing.

- Enjoy your surroundings when fishing, but be sure to keep your eye on your bobber.

- Don't take fishing too seriously; it is to be enjoyed.

- If the fish don't bite on your favorite lake, try a different lake.

- The words Gone Fishing on a closed business door are both respected and understood.

Other things to do when the chores are done:

- Take up a hobby to give your mind a rest from work—hiking, sewing, weaving, carving, writing poetry, or fixing an old engine.

What it is doesn't matter. What's important is taking an interest in something beyond your work.

- Go for a swim in a nearby lake on a hot evening in July, after the milking is done and there is still a couple hours of daylight. Take the whole family.

- Go to a polka dance. Dance the schottische, an old-time waltz, and the flying Dutchman. Dance every dance. Your troubles will lift with each beat, and you return home exhausted but refreshed.

- Learn how to play a guitar.

- Never be ashamed of doing nothing from time to time. We all need a break from our work.

Time

Rural people see time differently than their city cousins, whose lives often revolve around clocks and watches. Nature has its own clock, its own way of recording time.

- Time is the changing of the seasons, the first flock of geese in the spring, the call of the whip-poor-will on a hot summer evening, the sound of crickets in early fall, the silence of winter.

- Time is sunrise and sunset, when the corn is planted and the tomatoes are ready for canning, when the moon is full, and when there is no moon at all.

- Time is when the children are ready to leave home, when your hair turns gray and it takes twice as long to do something than when you were younger.

- Time is experience and wisdom, yesterday and tomorrow. Time is right now, this moment.

- Time is not the same as money, as some would suggest.

- Today is the tomorrow you worried about yesterday.

- Be on time, even a little early, if possible—no matter if you are going to church or to an ice cream social. Set all your clocks and watches ahead fifteen minutes to make sure you will always be on time. By doing this, you will have a time cushion, but you will never know exactly what time it is, for clocks and watches tend to gain and lose. Setting your clocks ahead will assure that you and your spouse will have something to discuss—"What time do you think it really is?"

- We all have the same number of hours in each day. Why do some of us run out of time sooner than others?

Take Time...

- To discover your family's roots—where your parents were born and what their growing-up years were like. Learn about your grandparents and their parents. What were their stories? To know who we are and where we are headed, we must know where we've been—we must know our family roots.

- To do nothing. To sit quietly. To clear your mind. Set aside the clutter of the day's activity and allow your mind to go blank. Do this several times a day.

- To dream. Dream about what might be, what will never be, and what shouldn't be. Too much doing with too little dreaming leads to boredom.

- To hear your daughter practicing scales on an old piano that has been in your family for three generations. Tell her she's doing well.

- To listen for a hoot owl far off in the woods to the north, the call of a sandhill crane in the marsh by the river, the low rumble of thunder on a hot, humid night in August.

- To listen for the quiet *dong, dong* of the bell on the neighbor's cow in night pasture, the chirping of hundreds of crickets on a warm night in early September, the laughter of children playing in the schoolyard just down the road.

- To listen for the sound of a church bell announcing the beginning of services, for the roar of a snowplow grinding along your drifted road.

- To listen to a robin's song in early spring, waves lapping on the shore of a lake, the creaking of an empty barn on a windy day, a word of praise from your mother-in-law, the cooing of a two-month-old baby.

- To listen to the gentle lowing of a cow for her newborn calf.

- To listen to the snapping and cracking of a stick of pinewood in your stove, for the lonesome whistle of a locomotive as it approaches country road crossings.

　　　　Rural Wit and Wisdom

- To paint a picture, sit under an oak tree on a sunny day, watch the sun set, smell an apple blossom, or play with a grandchild.

Do Something Different

Doing something different from the routine of everyday life gives us a new perspective, wakes us up, shows us the familiar in new ways, and helps us appreciate what we have.

- Climb a mountain. It doesn't have to be a tall one, just tall enough so you see over the tops of the trees and the roads and the fields that spread out below you.

- Go barefoot for an hour. Walk in the grass and allow it to sneak up between your toes. Feel the coolness on a hot summer day.

- Learn some words in another language. The more you know another language, the better you will understand your own.

- Listen to classical music, country tunes, rock, rap—whatever you've decided you don't like.

- Plant some Mexican corn that grows twenty feet tall and a few hills of squash that can weigh upward of two hundred pounds. When your brother-in-law asks, "Why?" answer, "Why not?"

- Spend a day a month volunteering at your local historical society.

- Spend an evening with a neighbor's aging parent, so they can have some time to themselves.

- Stand on the shores of Lake Superior in a November storm, when the wind sends mountainous waves crashing on the shore, causing the ore-boat captains to have second thoughts about their chosen careers.

- Take a canoe ride on a quiet lake. Rest the paddle and drift.

- Travel to another country. Avoid comparing what you see with what you have at home. See what you see for what it is, not how it is better or worse than something with which you are familiar.

- Visit a big city. Look to the top of the tall buildings, and do not care what others may think about your gazing. Watch the city at night, the thousands of bright lights everywhere, and wonder what the view must have been before electricity. Listen to the sounds of the city, the sirens and impatient car horns, the roar of truck engines and the clatter of commuter trains. Walk on a busy street among the hundreds of people hurrying this way and that, most with serious, determined looks on their faces.

• Visit Canada. Spend a night in Whitehorse, Yukon Territory, and become acquainted with the Alaskan Highway.

• Volunteer at your local library.

• Volunteer at your local school—help a youngster improve his reading skills, help another with her arithmetic.

• Walk on an Atlantic Ocean beach. Look for seashells. Listen to the surf that never stops, even when there is no wind. Look to the horizon and wonder what your ancestors must have felt when they landed in this country, on these shores, and realized that they would likely never return to their place of birth.

• Write a few lines of poetry. It doesn't matter if the words rhyme or not. What matters is that you express your feelings, which is the real stuff of poetry.

5

Family

Families have been central to rural life from the time when the first settlers arrived in the heartland to the present. Early farms, as well as many today, are family enterprises. The entire family works together, everyone with a task and a responsibility, from the youngest to the oldest.

On the farm where I grew up, the first job, when you were about four or five years old, was to fill the ever-empty wood box in the kitchen. As you got older, you graduated to feeding the chickens and gathering eggs—assuming that you had younger brothers and sisters to take over what was previously your responsibility. From the chickens you moved to carrying water and feed to the hogs—usually not a pleasant job, as the five-gallon buckets of water were heavy and the hogs were an unruly bunch, quick to fight over what you poured into their trough. Moving up the ladder of responsibility, the next rung took you to the barn, helping with the barn chores, first feeding the calves, then milking cows, forking hay from the haymow, tossing silage down from the silo, and shoveling manure. These latter chores were of the highest order; you looked forward to doing them and felt proud when your father tapped you on the shoulder one day and said, "How'd you like to help with the barn chores." Once your father determined you were ready, you did the task to the best of your ability. You not only learned how to do the work—learning how to milk a cow by hand took a little learning, forking hay was no great challenge, neither was shoveling manure—you did it without complaining.

Chores were family responsibilities. If you didn't do your chores, then someone else in the family had to do them. Sometimes you traded jobs. You fed the chickens for your brother so he could spend time with a school friend. Trading jobs was okay, as long as the work got done and was done properly.

Our father was a stickler for doing jobs right. He also, too often in my brothers' and my estimation, set the bar too high—he expected a level of excellence that exceeded our abilities. He not only wanted the job done, but he wanted it done with perfection—whether it was pitching hay, shoveling manure, or pounding a nail in a board that had come loose in the calf pen. For Pa, good enough was not good enough. He was always pushing us to do better. He wanted us to do more than we thought we could do. As I look back at those lessons now, I realize what he was doing. Most of us are capable of doing more than we think we can—and, alas, many of us will accept "good enough" when we could

have done something that was special and well beyond an average job.

Our father also made us realize that our individual chores all contributed to the overall operation of the farm. If any one of us did not do our chores well, it affected everything else. All the duties on a farm are integral, each chore depending on the other—it took me a long time to realize that. For instance, a missed feeding of chickens and you found them in the hog yard scrounging for something to eat with a strong possibility of being killed by a hungry hog. Eggs not gathered regularly resulted in broken eggs and loss of egg money, which bought our groceries. Some rules we learned about chores:

- A chore done well often leads to a promotion to one with a greater level of responsibility.

- Do your chores well. Every job, no matter how menial, deserves to be done to a high level of perfection.

- Never complain about doing your chores (at least not in earshot of either parent).

Family

- Never forget to do your chores. It is inexcusable and the possible punishment is never discussed.

- Show up on time, every time, every day, including weekends. Animals eat on weekends, too.

- Take pride in doing your chores and feel privileged that you have chores to do. Not everyone has the opportunity.

Unspoken Family Rules

My mother and father were not much for reciting rules that my brothers and I should follow, but we knew what they were. Sometimes we learned them by example, but more often we learned them by doing something and then being reminded that "Our family doesn't do that," whatever "that" happened to be at the time. Some of these rules were:

- Accept those who are different from you.

- At family gatherings, never take the last piece of bread, the last hunk of chicken, the last few carrots in the bowl—unless you are encouraged to do so.

- Avoid complaining; especially avoid whining—no one likes to be around a whiner.

- Avoid cussing—at least within earshot of your parents.

- Avoid squabbles with your siblings—especially those that lead to fistfights.

- Don't yell.

- Be a good loser—no moping or self-pity.

- Be a humble winner—no loud celebrating.

- Care for others, especially those who have less than you.

- Chew with your mouth shut.

- Comb your hair.

- Cover your mouth when you cough.

- Don't forget that humor and laughter will trump grumpiness and seriousness every time.

- If you are a man or boy, always let a woman or a girl pass through a door ahead of you.

- Learn to listen, which is more than merely hearing.

- Leave some things alone—it will help you stay out of trouble.

- Listen to your teacher; respect her, too. Her job is a challenging one, and your cooperation will make it easier.

- Look a person in the eye when you talk with them.

- Never boast.

- Never, ever talk back to your parents.

- Remember to say please and thank-you at appropriate times.

- Remember that someone always has more talent than you.

- Respect those who are older than you.

- Save your money.

- Sit up straight—no slouching in your chair.

- Speak clearly. No mumbling.

- Stay clear of politics and religion when meeting with family, friends, and neighbors. Troublesome disagreements will be avoided.

- Try to do more for others than they do for you.

- Walk with your head up—makes you look confident.

- When you go inside a building, take off your cap. It doesn't matter if it's your school, your home, church, or the neighbor's kitchen—the moment you step through the door, remove whatever is on your head.

- Write a thank-you note when you receive a gift.

Family Togetherness

Our closest neighbors, the Millers, lived more than half a mile away, so in some respects we were isolated and only had each other. Our isolation brought us together as a family. So did knowing that the success of our farm depended on each of us doing our share and making our contribution to the overall effort. Some of what I learned about family follows:

- A family that plays together stays together.

- Families that work together learn the meaning of cooperation and respect.

- Family comes first, before work, ahead of

play, beyond everything else that may look so important at the time.

- Family is the most important of all society's institutions—may it always be so.

- Family members, when out in public, defend and support each other. If another kid picks on one of your brothers, you stand ready to defend your brother.

- Follow moderation in all things, except for family, care of the land, and concern for neighbors. In these matters, be excessive.

- When you are down-and-out, you can always return to your family.

Children

- A tired child is a good child. Children with chores to do don't have the time or the energy to get into trouble.

- Allow your children to be children. The childhood years are few: the adult years are many. Having chores to do is important; so is having time for play.

- Allow your children to grow up being who they are, not what you want them to be. Even if you try to do this, who you are will be reflected in the words and actions of your children.

- Children may ignore your advice, but they will never ignore your example. They notice how you treat animals, how you care for the crops, what you say about your neighbor, and what you think of rural life.

- Children who do not see love at home will have difficulty seeing it anywhere else.

- Grandchildren are wonderful reminders of the things you forgot about your own children or were too busy raising them to notice.

- Help your children see the importance of their name, and how once it is tarnished it will remain so, no matter how hard they work to make it otherwise.

- No matter how much you might think otherwise, you are your children's most important teacher.

- Show children, don't tell them. Show them the meaning of honesty, of caring and sharing, and concern for those who have less than you do—through your actions.

- Support your children's teacher. You and your children's teacher are a team. You need each other, but, more importantly, your children need parents and teachers working together.

- Talk to little children; listen to them, for their ideas are fresh. Watch them. Learn from them. They are real and experiencing life to the fullest.

- The two most important things we can give our children are roots as deep as the giant oaks and wings as strong as an eagle's.

- There is no better discipline than hoeing thistles in a cornfield for eight hours under a hot July sun. Something valuable is accomplished, too.

- There is no such thing as hugging a child too much.

- What a child learns at home will remain forever.

- When a child asks why, take time to answer, no matter how often the question is repeated.

- Your children can be your best teachers, especially in helping you become aware of what you take for granted: Why is the sky blue? Where do eggs come from? Where does the sun go at night? Why does it thunder? How can fish live in water?

6

For Good Health

Wisdom about health abounds in the heartland. Much of it is practical, down-to-earth, and as good advice today as it was one hundred fifty years ago, when doctors were scarce and a hospital was a day's trip or more away. Some of the advice may have had value in an earlier day, but is not something anyone would recommend now—for instance, filling a pillow with hops instead of feathers in order to sleep better. Some of the advice was silly; yet people swore by a particular practice's effectiveness. My grandmother insisted that when you had a fever, you went to bed and piled on the covers. The idea was to sweat out the fever. Some of the old treatments, such as drinking worm root tea to calm an upset stomach, worked because of the natural ingredients in the plant.

I don't recall anyone using words like "mental health" and "depression" when I was growing up. People said such things as "down in the dumps," "feeling blue," and "moody" to describe a woman's mental state. For men, the words were more likely "Something's wrong with Joe. He's not right these days," or "Ben's sure got ornery since his best cow died."

We knew that health was more than what happened to the body, and rural people had advice on what to do about it. Here are some suggestions.

Health Tips

- Avoid constantly looking for an ache or a pain. If you keep looking, you will likely find something, some kink, some difficulty on which to dwell and cause you to worry and take your mind away from more constructive things.

- Be careful about too much bathing. A bath on Saturday night, before going to town, is sufficient. Too much water will weaken you, sap the strength right out of your muscles. Consider how you feel when you go swimming. Most people are worn out. The same thing can happen to you if you spend too much time in a bathtub.

- Chew your food slowly.

- Don't feel guilty about leaning on your hoe or shovel from time to time and resting.

- Drink lots of water, especially on a hot day.

- Drink water fresh from a well. The less distance the water flows from its source to you, the better it tastes. The best water of all comes from a pump after it has been running for an hour or so, filling the cattle tank. All of the pipes are as cold as the water; the sweetness of well water is enhanced by its coldness.

- Go to bed early; get up early. The best hours of the day are before noon. The best hours of all are before breakfast.

- Horse liniment has wonderful qualities. Use it to treat various external injuries of your horses and to solve various internal problems as well. Same for humans. A strained muscle, a sore back? Rub on a little liniment. An upset stomach? A little liniment diluted in water will do wonders.

- If your chest is congested, rub on an ample amount of skunk grease. Pin a square of flannel to your underwear to keep the power of the skunk grease in rather than moving out. To dispel any disbelief, skunk grease bears none of the interesting aroma associated with its source. It has no smell whatever. Always keep a supply of skunk grease handy. In addition to its medicinal qualities, it makes a wonderful preservative for leather boots. Leather boots regularly treated with skunk grease will remain soft and pliable and become near waterproof.

- Keep a few bottles of beer in your refrigerator. Nothing tastes better at the end of a long, hot day in summer than a cold beer. Be careful of the beer you buy. The brands vary widely. Buy a local beer, one brewed in one of the little breweries that recently opened in your community. It generally has more flavor and gumption than the thinned-out national brands that claim low calories and offer little taste.

- Laugh when your uncle tells you that on the first warm days in spring at the lumber camp, the lumberjacks took off their underwear and piled it by the river's edge. When the bedbugs went for a drink, the lumberjacks quickly grabbed up their bug-free underwear and ran back to the bunkhouse.

- Learn something new every day. Learning is a key to a healthy mind.

- Learn to laugh again. Most of us have forgotten how. Try to laugh out loud at least once every day—several times, if possible. There is nothing more fulfilling than a good laugh, the kind that starts down in your belly and grows.

- Learn to laugh at yourself.

- Start each day by drinking a full glass of water.

- Stay out of taverns.

- Stop eating while you are still hungry.

- Walk whenever possible and wherever you can. You'll see more, learn more, have an opportunity to think more, and, besides, you'll feel better.

- Watch out for black wasps, the kind that builds a paperlike nest. They have the most wicked of bites and the fiercest of tempers. Avoid them.

- When you develop a bad cold, ease the symptoms by drinking a whiskey sling. Make a whiskey sling by pouring a shot of whiskey into a glass of hot water and adding a little lemon to help make the concoction go down easier. Repeat if necessary.

Food

Food has always been important—especially having enough of it. These days, the quality of the food we eat has taken center stage along with concerns for food safety, as huge amounts of food have been recalled from grocery stores and food processors because of contamination of various kinds. People are buying more of their food locally and supporting area farmers. Today, the idea of growing one's own food—doing some gardening—has become a popular notion. Country people have long known the importance of good, nourishing food. Farmers generally have large vegetable gardens, home orchards, and chicken flocks producing much of what they eat right at home.

- Avoid store-bought bread; there is no power in it. Make bread from flour purchased by the fifty-pound sack. The empty sack can be used for making dresses, towels, and sometimes stuffed animals.

- Eat food from the garden. In winter, eat canned or frozen food from the garden, stored potatoes from the cellar, sauerkraut from the crock, and meat from the smoked ham that hangs alongside the cellar steps. Enjoy fresh venison after deer-hunting season.

- Eat plain food.

- Eat your largest meal at noon. Call it dinner, not lunch. Lunch is what you eat after playing cards in the evening at a relative's home or what the neighbor serves after you help butcher a pig. Supper is what you eat in the early evening, when the outdoor work for the day is finished and before you do the evening chores.

- In July, search for wild black raspberries in the woods. Tolerate the mosquitoes and scratches, for the best berries are often in the deepest tangle of brush.

- Never criticize the cook or the cooking.

Sleep

- Avoid spending too much time in bed; after all, most people die there.

- Early to bed and early to rise probably won't increase your wealth or your wisdom, but it will do wonders for your health.

- Resist the temptation to dawdle in bed once you wake up. When you wake up, get up.

- Try to get eight hours of sleep; for some people a little more is necessary, for others a little less.

- Two hours of sleep before midnight are worth more than four hours after.

Curing Unhappiness

Feeling down and depressed is something that happens to many people, if not most, at one time or another. It doesn't matter if you live in the country or an urban area. Rural people have long known many approaches to dealing with what is commonly called unhappiness. Serious depression, that which goes well beyond unhappiness, requires medical attention and should be treated just as one would treat a serious physical problem.

To overcome unhappiness:

- Avoid assuming that if only the government, your spouse, the weather—you fill in the blank—would change, you would be a happier person.

- Discount believing that the more things you accumulate, the happier you'll be.

- Don't create problems when none exist.

- Don't make little problems into big problems.

- Enjoy the present rather than always looking for happiness in the future.

- Happiness often comes when we're not looking for it.

- It isn't how many times you fall that counts, but how many times you get back up.

- Life's journey is often two steps forward and one step back.

- Some of the best of what is next has been here all along.

- Smile more than frown.

- Worry about important things; the little things aren't worth the effort worrying requires.

For the Bad Days

When everything seems to be coming apart in your life, when what you hoped for didn't happen, when your spouse does something to disappoint you, when just about everything appears dark and gloomy:

- Bake bread from scratch.

- Go ice fishing. Sitting on a frozen lake in winter with a few old friends provides a wonderful opportunity to swap stories, and, in the quiet of a dark and dreary winter day, reflect on life. Occasionally you will catch a fish—a northern pike or perhaps a perch or a bluegill. The taste of fish from a frozen lake is beyond description.

- Scrub the kitchen floor, on your hands and knees, with a brush. Anger, frustration, whatever is bothering you will disappear—and you'll have a clean floor, too.

- Vow to once a week set aside a few minutes to

do nothing, to think about nothing, to worry about nothing.

- Walk around your land, all the way around the boundaries. You could tell your spouse you are checking the fences. Maybe you are, but not the ones with fence posts.

- Walk in the woods on a quiet morning when the only sound is that of the birds in the treetops.

- Whittle. You don't have to make anything. A pile of wood shavings on the floor is an accomplishment, especially when everything seems to be going wrong.

- Write in a journal. Jot down your feelings, your unhappiness, and your anger. Pull no punches. When you're finished, you'll feel as if your problems have now been transferred to paper and are no longer yours.

Complaining

Complaining seems to be a part of human nature. Some people wouldn't be happy unless they had something to complain about, or so it appears. They complain about the weather, their neighbors, their relatives, the government—just about everything. For them the glass is always half empty.

- Facing a problem head-on is far easier than complaining about it.

- For some people, finding the negative in life and complaining about it is easier than discovering the positive and applauding it.

- Take time to look at a daisy. Daisies grow on dry land and wet, alongside highways and open fields. They come in blue and white, yellow and pink. They are often chewed off, clipped off, stomped on, and picked. Yet they always come back, in full color, with nary a complaint.

- The world is what we make it. What is important is how we react to the world that we see, rather than merely complaining.

What-Ifs

Many of us spend far too much time fretting over what might have been if only we had done something differently. For example, what if we had:

harvested the oat crop a day earlier and avoided the hailstorm that destroyed most of it?

- held our temper when junior did something wrong?

- planted more acres of corn because the crop we raised turned out so well?

- remembered to close the barnyard gate so we didn't have to spend an hour rounding up the heifers?

We also project our what-ifs into the future, allowing them to take up much of our thinking time and disturb our mental state.

- What if a cow gets sick?

- What if the meadow down by the creek floods this year, as it did five years ago?

- What if the old tractor doesn't make it through the summer?

- What if the price of milk goes down?

- What if this year the old windmill needs replacing?

- What if we don't get enough rain this summer?

- What if we have an early frost in the fall, as we had last year?

One way to handle the what-ifs is to consider the worst possible thing that could happen if the what-if comes true and what we could do about it. Thinking this way, many of our what-ifs disappear.

7

Home-Grown Food

The idea of buying vegetables from a grocery story never crossed my mother's mind. She tended a large garden that grew in a plot behind our farmhouse and next to the woodlot that stretched to the north. The garden contained about every vegetable that would grow in central Wisconsin—several rows of sweet corn, tomatoes, potatoes, green beans, peas, carrots, and cabbage—vegetables that could be canned or stored during the long winter months. Lesser vegetables like eggplant and peppers were there too, but in shorter rows. Of course, pumpkins and squash had their place—they could be stored in our dirt-floor cellar until Christmas and sometimes a little after. Watermelons were a favorite for my brothers and me. We had a long row of them. When they were ripe, we immediately ate them.

Those we didn't eat we stored in the granary's oat bin to keep from freezing. Ma also grew leaf lettuce and radishes that we harvested and ate as soon as they were ready in the spring.

My father cultivated the garden a few times with a one-horse cultivator—the rows were forty inches apart—and later with the tractor. From my mother's perspective, he never did the cultivating properly. The heavy-footed horses and the tractor's tires flattened some of my mother's favorite vegetables, and my father heard about it. But overall, the garden grew well. Here is a little garden wisdom that I've learned over the years:

- Take time to plan your garden each year. The plan doesn't have to be fancy—the back of an envelope is fine—but do some planning.

- Plant your garden as early as possible. Depending on how far north you are, some of the early crops such as radishes, onions, lettuce, peas, and early potatoes can go in the ground in late April or early May. Leave behind the notion that you must plant the entire garden at once. It's best to plant it over several weeks, with the last crops planted being the late sweet corn and tomatoes that can't stand even a hint of late spring frost before the leaves curl up, turn brown, and die. If the ground is too cold—in the midfifties—seeds such as squash, pumpkins, and watermelons won't germinate, so watch the spring temperatures and plant accordingly. In most years, much of my garden is usually planted by Memorial Day.

- Plant tomatoes in a different place each year. By doing this you can help to control tomato blight and other tomato diseases.

- Keep the cucumbers away from the squash, gourds, and zucchini plants. These more aggressive vine plants will overrun the cucumbers, and you'll have next to no yield of cucumbers.

- Keep the sweet corn away from the popcorn. They'll cross-pollinate and you'll have both strange sweet corn and unusual popcorn.

- Start tomatoes indoors six to eight weeks before you set them in your garden. That way, your tomatoes will have a good start by the time you plant them out. Don't be too fussy about planting the tomato seeds. Dump some clean potting soil in a garden pot. Sprinkle on the garden seeds. Cover the seeds with a little soil and then put the pot in a south-facing window. Keep the soil moist, and in a week or so little tomato plants will peek out. Leave them in the garden pots until garden-planting time. Don't worry much about thinning. The main thing is to keep them watered. Once they are up and growing and the daytime temperatures are in the sixties or warmer, make sure to put the little tomato plants, still in their pots, outside so they can toughen a bit before you plant them in your garden.

- Plant the tomatoes so they are open to any breeze that flows across your garden. The summer breezes help to dry out the plants from the morning dews and summer showers and keep down the pesky tomato blight. One way to assure the tomatoes are out in the open is to plant peas and lettuce near them. When the peas and lettuce are harvested, pull the plants, leaving more room for the tomatoes.

- Plant some marigolds in your garden, at least a row or two. They tend to keep insects away and provide a nice floral display from late summer until frost.

- Plant raspberry plants where you can cultivate around them. This you will need to do regularly throughout the growing season, or one day you'll discover that your entire garden has become a raspberry bed.

- Plant several kinds of squash. I especially enjoy buttercup and butternut. I also plant several hills of the old-fashioned Hubbard squash and a few hills of acorn squash.

- Cauliflower is a bit fussy to grow, so I leave it alone.

- Broccoli and Brussels sprouts generally do well. We enjoy eating them fresh. I also start them from seeds indoors, the same time I start the tomatoes, following the same guidelines.

- Don't overplant zucchini squash. Three or four hills should be enough. If you plant more, given half a chance and a decent growing year, you will have enough zucchini to feed everyone in your township. Try new ways to fix this often maligned vegetable. It is a wonderful ingredient for baking, such as in zucchini chocolate brownies or zucchini bread, which our grandchildren will eat before cookies. Zucchini also goes well in salads and stir-fries. Here is Ruth's recipe for zucchini bread:

Ruth's Zucchini Bread

2 cups zucchini, peeled and grated
3 eggs, beaten
1 cup vegetable oil
2 cups sugar
2 teaspoons vanilla
3 cups flour
1 teaspoon baking soda
½ teaspoon baking powder
1 teaspoon salt
1 teaspoon ground cinnamon

1. Preheat oven to 325°F. Grease and flour 3 pans (7½ inch x 3¾ inch x 2¼ inch).

2. In a bowl, beat eggs. Add oil, sugar, zucchini, and vanilla. Mix well.

3. Sift and mix the remaining dry ingredients together.

4. Add dry ingredients to wet ingredients, and mix until thoroughly blended. Divide mixture among the pans. Bake 45 to 50 minutes,

until bread is brown and pulls away from sides of pan.

Note: You can double the recipe if you have a large bowl for mixing the wet and dry mixtures together. Make sure the flour is mixed well with the other ingredients. The expanded recipe makes 6 to 7 loaves.

- Plant some rutabagas; a short row will give you enough for vegetable soup. Nothing tastes better than a rutabaga or two in a kettle of soup, cooked with pork hocks, or even cooked by themselves and served like potatoes. Be sure to eat all the stored rutabagas before the following spring. A spoiled rutabaga competes well with a rotten egg. A couple bushels of spoiled rutabagas will give your house an aroma that will live with you for months—like an unwelcome guest who never bathes, except much worse.

- Plant a long row of onions. I plant half the row to red onions, the other half to yellow onions. The easiest way to plant onions is to buy onion sets—little onions—at a garden supply store and then set them in a little trench you make along the row. Cover the sets completely, but make sure the growing end is pointed upward when you set them out.

- Plant some dill. A few hills will provide what is necessary for dill pickles. Dill can be planted directly from seeds and provides a wonderful aroma when you pinch a leaf while it is growing.

- Don't forget a few hills of gourds. A couple or three hills is all you need, as gourd vines seem to do the best of all the vine crops. In a good year, they'll climb over the top of the pumpkins and even up and over the sweet corn, making a tangled mess. But all anger toward this competitive vine disappears when you find the many multicolored and multishaped gourds in the fall.

- Don't forget cabbage. You'll need lots of it if you plan to make sauerkraut. Cabbage seeds can also be started indoors, about the same time you start tomato seeds. Nothing tastes better on a cool day in autumn than homemade sauerkraut. Here's how to make it:

Homemade Sauerkraut

White cabbage, large heads (5 pounds of cabbage will make about 1 gallon of sauerkraut)

Non-iodized salt (Coarse pickling salt is preferred. The purpose of the salt is to draw the juice out of the cabbage so it will ferment.)

A large, sharp knife to shred the cabbage if a kraut cutter is not available

An earthenware crock from 2½ to 20 gallons, depending on how much sauerkraut you wish to make

A covering consisting of several layers of coarse cheese cloth or muslin (This will be placed between the cut cabbage and a china plate.)

A china plate large enough to cover the cabbage and also fit within the crock

A rock or clean brick to weigh down the plate (The covering and the weight are used to bring the brine to the surface of the shredded kraut. It is important to keep oxygen out of the crock as it will cause spoilage. Keep all metal away from the process.)

1. Remove the coarse outer leaves from the cabbage. Do not wash the heads—the natural yeasts found there are necessary for fermentation to take place.

2. Cut the heads into halves and then quarters. Slice cabbage to obtain shreds as long as possible and about the thickness of a nickel (1/16 inch).

3. Place the shredded cabbage in layers in the crock. For every inch or so of layered cabbage, sprinkle 2½ tablespoons of salt.

4. After every 2 or 3 layers, tamp the shredded cabbage with a clean piece of wood or a glass jar.

5. Fill the crock within 4 or 5 inches of the top. Position the cloth covering over the kraut and lap it over the edge of the container. Place the snug-fitting china plate on the cloth.

6. Finally, put the weight on the plate. The action of the salt will draw the juice out of the cabbage and make brine, which will rise to the top. Mold may appear on the top of the brine. Remove it daily.

7. Store the fermenting kraut in a well-ventilated place with a temperature about 60°F–65°F.

8. In 3 to 5 days, remove the cover and check the progress. Some discoloration due to spoilage may occur on the top inch or so. Remove it. Rinse the cloth clean before replacing it.

9. The kraut should be ready for eating in about a month to 6 weeks. It will keep indefinitely in the crock as long as the top is not exposed to air. The fermented sauerkraut may be removed from the crock, placed in freezer

bags, and stored in the refrigerator for several months. It may also be canned or frozen.

- Grow some flowers in your garden. Gladiolas, zinnias, and marigolds (mentioned earlier) are good choices. So are sunflowers. Plant a row of sunflowers along the edge of your garden. They grow fast, and soon yellow faces will greet you each day, besides providing much-appreciated bird food.

- As you sow the seeds for each row in your garden, push a stick into the ground at the end of it. Black locust sticks work well because they don't rot easily and thus can be used year after year. Fasten the empty seed packet to the stick; then you'll remember what you planted.

- If you are a bit more organized, you may want to create a map of your garden as you plant it. Your plan was a guide; the map is the real thing. In this way, you'll know for sure what is planted where, even when the wind and rain tear away the empty seed packets fastened to the black locust sticks.

- Include potatoes in your garden, at least three kinds. Early red ones for eating with fresh peas, late white ones for storing in the cellar, and russet potatoes for baking.

- Plant carrots with the radishes. After the radishes are harvested, the carrots will flourish, requiring little or no thinning.

- Grow at least three kinds of sweet corn—very early, midsummer, and late. That way you'll have fresh sweet corn for much of the summer.

- After harvesting the early sweet corn, cut the remaining corn plants into small pieces and leave them in the garden for mulch. Cutting down the corn plants allows sunlight to reach plants in your garden that the corn may have shaded.

- Leave the tops of the beets, radishes, and carrots in the garden for mulch.

- In the late summer, when sections of your garden have been harvested, work up the soil and plant winter wheat or rye. Next spring, when you plow your garden, you'll discover that the winter green manure crop has grown several inches and will provide needed organic material for your garden soil. Many gardens, especially where the soil is sandy, are severely lacking in organic material.

- Toss your wood ashes on your garden, especially where you plan to plant potatoes. Wood

Rural Wit and Wisdom

ash has a goodly amount of potash in it, something potatoes need to produce well.

- You can bury a lot of troubles digging in your garden.

- All gardeners know better than other gardeners.

- Gardening is one way to be close to the earth, in more ways than you could imagine.

Other Gardening Thoughts

- Plant some rhubarb on the edge of your garden. The old-timers called it pieplant—it does make a wonderfully tasty pie. Rhubarb is the first garden plant to poke out its nose after winter and a few sunny, warm days. In addition to pie, it makes great sauce. My dad always said that rhubarb was a blood purifier; eaten in the spring, it cleanses the body from the accumulations of a long winter. It requires almost no tending and comes back each spring with elephant ear–size leaves and beautiful, reddish-pink stalks. It is the stalks that you eat; the leaves contain an organic poison. Here is Ruth's recipe for rhubarb cream pie:

Rhubarb Cream Pie

3 eggs
1⅓ cups sugar
¼ cup flour
1 teaspoon cinnamon
4 cups rhubarb cut into ½-inch pieces

1. Beat eggs slightly in large bowl.

2. Mix sugar, flour, and cinnamon together.

3. Add to eggs and mix until smooth.

4. Add rhubarb and mix until rhubarb is co

5. Pour into a pastry-lined 9-inch pie she

6. Dot with 2 tablespoons butter.

7. Cover with top crust, making sure t openings in the top crust.

8. Brush top crust with milk and spri sugar.

9. Bake at 425°F for 15 minutes, for 30 to 35 minutes. Crust sh brown and crisp. Use knife to te set. Knife comes out clean.

- Set out a strawberry patch. ries three times a day in June flakes for breakfast, in stra

for dinner, and as strawberries and cream or
…aybe strawberry pie for supper. Make a straw-
…ry sandwich for lunch anytime. To make a
…vberry sandwich, pick five or six large, lush
…erries. Place them on a thick slice of but-
…memade bread. Smash the strawberries
…nner fork, sprinkle on a little sugar,
… second slice of bread. Eat hardy.

…orseradish. On the home farm,
…radish back of the chicken
…mother had planted a few
…s, in their everyday scratch-
…down but didn't seem to
… at all.

…m strawberries, wild
… grow wild on your

…ur garden.
…p of the
…rooms
…ake

53

Here are the directions for making a broom:

1. Start with the heads from 10 or 12 broomcorn plants. Comb out the seeds that are on
   the ends of the bristles. Save the seeds for the
   birds and some for planting next year.

2. Fasten the heads together, leaving the bristles
   free. Hay wire or any other wire (like picture
   frame wire) that won't break when you twist it
   together will work fine. Three or four pieces of
   wire should be enough. Slip a piece of leather
   thong, 4 or 5 inches long, under the top wire
   before you tighten it. The leather thong will
   provide a way to hang up your little broom. A
   leather shoelace makes a perfect thong. With
   a sharp knife, square off the ends of the bristles so they are all the same length. You have
   made a whisk broom for cleaning in the corners of your home, brushing off the furniture,
   and cleaning the trunk of your car.

Variation. Follow steps one and two until you
get to the place where you are tightening the
wire around the broomcorn heads. This time,
fasten the broomcorn heads around a handle
made from a ¾-inch stick about 18 inches
long. Black locust works especially well, but
almost any wood will suffice—willow and ash

are also choices. With a jackknife, cut a few grooves in the part of the stick where you will fasten the broomcorn heads. This will help prevent the broomcorn from slipping off the stick when everything dries out and shrinks a little. Now you have what some people call a fireplace broom. A longer handle and a few more broomcorn heads and you'll have a regular, full-size broom. Try different lengths of handles and different amounts of broomcorn. Great fun for a rainy day in fall, with the rain splashing on the shed roof.

8

Little Things

As our daily lives become increasingly more complicated, relish the little things—the quiet pleasures that make each day a little more exciting and worthwhile. Some of the little things may take you back to an earlier day, when your life may have been a bit less difficult. Savor little things to provide some balance to the present-day, loud, cluttered, and increasingly electronic world.

Some Little Things

- Appreciating a warm floor to put your feet on when the temperature outside is below zero. Remember the days of your youth when you woke up in an unheated bedroom and the floor was as cold as the ice on a frozen lake.

- Discovering that a new recipe you tried turned out better than you expected.

- When shopping for something you need, you discover it is on sale.

- Enjoying a fountain pen for writing. There is something about the flow of ink on paper that adds to the experience of writing, beyond the message you are trying to convey.

- Enjoying a good cup of coffee in the morning that gives you the gumption to face the day, no matter how many problems and challenges lie in wait.

- Enjoying hearing a teenager admit that you, as a parent, are right about something.

- Having freshly ground pepper for every meal. Nothing improves the taste of good food more. Avoid salt.

- Having the opportunity to read a book without interruption.

- Hearing a word of praise for a job well done.

- Owning a comfortable chair. You only need one, and when you find it, keep it. If your spouse tells you it has become shabby and unsightly, resist the temptation to buy a new one. It often takes years to break in a chair. If an ugly chair becomes a problem for appearances, such as when the preacher is planning a visit, toss a bedspread over it. When the preacher leaves, yank off the cover and sink back into your chair and be comfortable. Hard to be comfortable when the preacher is visiting, anyway.

- Owning shoes that fit, even if you must pay a few extra dollars for them. There is nothing that contributes more to a sour disposition than sore feet.

- Pulling the first radish from your garden in spring or picking the first lush red strawberry from your strawberry bed.

- Reading a good book, slowly, allowing the words to roam around in your mind and stir up your thinking and your feelings.

- Realizing that most little things that make day-to-day life more enjoyable do not involve money.

- Receiving a bouquet of flowers you didn't expect.

- Remembering that being comfortable is more important than being stylish.

- Sleeping well at night—it can make all the difference in your disposition and attitude toward life.

- Taking a fifteen minute nap at midday, without guilt.

- Talking with a three-year-old, especially if he or she is your grandchild. Listening carefully to the words and the perspectives and wisdom. Three-year-olds move to the core of matters in their thinking and in their communication.

9

Practical Matters

When you are five miles from town, you learn how to fix things yourself—a broken farm implement, a leaking pipe, even a sick animal. You learn how to do things in the most practical way possible, because you don't have time or money to take the long way around for doing something.

General Tips

- Carry a jackknife. One blade should have enough edge so you can sharpen a pencil, do a little whittling, or peel an apple. The other blade is best left dull. Use the dull blade for scraping grease off machinery, slitting open your mail, or, in a pinch, serving as a screwdriver.

- In another pocket, carry a pair of pliers. With a jackknife and pliers you can make assorted repairs and work yourself out of many difficulties. A pair of pliers can do everything from cutting wire to pounding in a staple on a fence where the wire has popped loose.

- Carry a few eight-penny nails in your pocket as well. There is always a loose board that needs fixing. You can even use a nail as a staple to fasten wire to a fence post. Just drive it in partway and bend it over. Not a pretty sight, but it works.

- Keep an ample supply of nuts, bolts, screws, and nails of various sizes on hand. This will save many trips to town.

- Every farmer knows to have wrenches of various sizes on hand, including ratchet as well as box wrenches. These days it's also important to have at least one set of wrenches in metric sizes.

- A midsized crescent wrench carried in your pocket, or in the tractor's toolbox, will often save a trip back to the shed where you keep your wrenches.

- Have screwdrivers of every size, both flat end and Phillips. Screwdrivers come in handy for all kinds of things, from loosening and tightening screws, of course, to digging and prying and getting into tight places.

- Buy an extendable magnet, the kind that's about the size of a pencil. When you drop a nut or a washer in a place too tight for your fingers, the magnet will go far in saving your religion.

- Carry a pocket watch. It used to be that you could buy a good Pocket Ben for a dollar; that was the case for many years. They cost more now, but serve as well. A watch on your wrist is always in trouble. When you are splitting wood, you shake the bejeebers out of it, sometimes even shaking off the hands. Nothing worse than a watch that keeps good time but can't tell anyone. A pocket watch is always there, ticking away. Of course, you have to fish for it to find out the time, but there's no reason to look at your watch more than a couple times a day anyway—at dinnertime and at suppertime. Grandchildren like pocket watches, too. They put the watch to their ear and listen to the ticktock. One of Grandpa's many mysteries.

- Carry a small notebook and a pencil in your pocket. Never can tell when you will think of something worthy of noting or, even more important, when you will want to jot down something that needs doing so you don't forget it.

- Keep the chimneys on your kerosene lamps clean. A smoky chimney blocks out at least half the lamp's light.

- Learn to fix things yourself. You have both the satisfaction of doing it your way and the knowledge that you've saved some money.

- Know when to ask someone else to fix something for you. What is broken a little may be broken a lot when you start fixing it.

- If you're eating an apple and find a worm, be thankful it isn't half a worm.

- Estimate the amount of time you believe it will take to complete a task. Then double it. Almost everything takes longer than you think it will—a lot longer.

- Try new ideas, but go slow. Let a new idea roll around in your head for a couple of weeks, maybe even longer, before acting on it.

- If you need to measure something and you don't have a ruler, use a dollar bill. It's six inches long.

- To gauge distance, measure your stride; for many people, it is about a yard. Then walk, counting your steps. You will have a rough estimate of the number of yards you've walked. Rural people call this "pacing off a distance."

- Measure twice, cut once. Good advice for a lot more than carpentry.

- There is nothing more practical than a good theory.

- Keep things simple. They'll get complicated enough, soon enough, without you intending that they should.

- Never trust a barn cat.

- Don't turn your back on a billy goat.

- Don't make a pet of a pig; it will spoil your taste for bacon.

- Never make a mistake, but learn from those that you do make.

Clothing

- Wear simple clothing. A cotton shirt and a couple pair of bib overalls are about all a man needs, except for going to church. New overalls for trips to town on Saturday night. Faded overalls for work.

- A woman needs several good aprons, the kind that come up to the neck and extend below the dress and have a couple of pockets to carry safety pins and a handkerchief. A good apron protects a dress from spills and splashes. It's also a good place to dry your hands, gather eggs, wipe away a child's tears, or wave with when you want Joe's attention in the back forty.

- Never buy a shirt that doesn't have a pocket. It is where you can keep your notebook and pencil.

- Always wear long-sleeved shirts. They protect from mosquitoes and other pests, prevent excessive sunburn, and can be rolled up when the weather is warm. Short-sleeved shirts have no such multiple uses.

- Avoid wearing a necktie. It cuts off circulation to the brain and thus prevents clear thinking.

- Don't wear pants with a belt. The tightness around the stomach prevents good digestion.

- Consider wearing suspenders, big wide ones that don't cut into your shoulders. Suspenders will keep up your pants no matter if your middle has expanded a bit and your pants want to slip below the bulge.

- Never wear short pants. They were made for people who never walk through wild berry patches or wet, knee-high grass.

- Don't go outside without wearing your shirt. If God had meant for you to run around naked, you would have been born that way.

- Buy handkerchiefs that are at least eighteen inches square; they are usually blue or red. Besides taking care of your nose, these more substantial pieces of cloth work well to clean your glasses and rub the sweat from your brow. They also work well for signaling—someone waving a big red handkerchief is difficult to overlook.

- Wear a straw hat in summer and a wool cap with earflaps in winter. When your head is cool, your body is cool. When your head is warm, your body is warm. It's as simple as that.

- Own a sturdy pair of leather gloves. They help prevent many scratches and scrapes and prevent blisters early in the season, before the callouses on your winter hands have fully developed.

- Wear strong leather boots that come up above your ankles. This will keep sand from getting into your shoes—very uncomfortable—as well as protect your ankles when you are walking on uneven surfaces.

10

Taking Life as It Comes

Rural people have long known that too much of anything, whether it is work, rainfall, or a city relative's visit, is not good and can lead to problems. Also, because so much of what occurs in the country is caused by something beyond a person's control—weather, markets, sick animals—flexibility is needed.

Take Life as It Comes

- Answer an ad for a surprise offer. Don't be disappointed when the item arrives and is not up to your expectations—be surprised.

- Appreciate the value of looking forward to something as you enjoy what you are doing now.

- Avoid crowds, loud talking, big cities, and boastful people.

- Avoid looking at things as other people say you should see them. You are entitled to your own view.

- Avoid using the word *impossible*, except when it fits.

- Be optimistic. Even when the bottom leaves of the corn are drying and the haymows are only half as full, there is always next year with its promise and mystery, its hope and anticipation. And if not next year, the year after that.

- Being spiritual and being religious are not the same. Some spiritual people will have nothing to do with organized religion.

- Better to downplay success than gloat about it. Even when you are having a good year—the rains have come regularly, the first cutting of hay was tall and lush, and the corn crop looks promising—it is better to reply, when asked how things are going, with "Could be worse" than saying something like "Outstanding!" or

"Couldn't be better." You just never know when a hailstorm will ruin the corn crop or lightning will strike the barn and burn it to the ground.

- Cherish the past. Anticipate the future. Enjoy the present.

- Do it right the first time.

- Doing things "straight" leads to clear thinking and points you in an uncluttered direction. Doing things straight means building a straight fence, shocking grain in straight rows, plowing a straight furrow, and planting corn rows that run north and south, or east and west, never on the diagonal. But sometimes circling is the better way to go. For instance, when trying to convince a neighbor of something, it is usually better to circle around the topic a couple of times than to blurt out what you have on your mind. A good place to start the conversation is talking about the weather, then move on to the crops and the cows and the terrible state of the world—then ease into the topic you really want to talk about. Your neighbor will know what you are doing. You'll both enjoy the process, even though it takes lots of time and often doesn't lead to mind changing. Except, sometimes it does.

- Don't be too taken by churches and preachers. God is in many places; a church or other religious building is but one of them. Being religious Monday through Saturday is more important than being religious on Sunday. It's easy on Sunday, not so easy the rest of the week.

- Dream big dreams, but be careful; consider the consequences if your dreams come true.

- Enjoy being alone; enjoy being with others.

- Enjoy what you have. Some people have more; many people, less.

- If you don't feel like smiling, smile anyway. People will think you're having a good time.

- No matter how fast things change, hold on to a few things that don't.

- It is often better to see things as they are than to try and change them.

- It takes time for the mud to settle in a murky stream, just as it takes time for the mud to settle in our daily lives.

- Keep up with what is happening in the world. Read more than one newspaper, watch more than one TV news report, and listen to a variety of radio programs. It is always good to have a second opinion, especially when it comes to farming, politics, and religion.

- Know your history—where you were born, where you grew up—but don't dwell on it. Only you can decide what view to take on your past, what to share, what to leave behind.

- Living in the past can be as harmful to your mental state as living in the future. Both are important places to visit, but don't forget about the present.

- Remember to listen for the whispers and look in the shadows.

- Success is not forever.

- Tackle a small problem when you first notice it. A small problem ignored can become a large problem not easily solved. The tendency is to overlook the little problems until they become big and then panic and declare a crisis.

- Those who are given much are expected to give much back in return.

- Realize that joy can be found almost everywhere, if you take time to look.

Growing Older

Whether we like it or not, we are all growing older. It is our attitude toward aging that generally makes the difference as the years accumulate and we remain joyful or not.

- Age really doesn't matter unless you're cheddar cheese. For cheddar cheese, the older the better.

- As we grow older, we tend to forget things that happened and remember things that didn't.

- Be careful of the past; it always looks better than it was.

- Being alive is not the same as not being dead.

- Being old is better than being dead. But never having been dead, I can't speak with much confidence.

- Call an old friend; somebody you knew when you were in high school. You'll both feel better after the conversation.

- Cherish the memories of yesterday. Dream big dreams about tomorrow. Live happily today.

- Curiosity may have killed the cat, but it is one of the things that keeps older people young.

Rural Wit and Wisdom

- Do the best you can with what you've got.

- Every day is a good day; some days are just better than others.

- Everyone's life is special, no matter how old or young you are—or think you are.

- Expect little and then be pleased when you receive more.

- Fellow said he was born with nothing and still had most of it left.

- How come common sense isn't so common anymore?

- If it's not bothering you, leave it alone.

- If you have a why to live, you can handle most any how.

- It's never too late.

- It's not over until it's over, except when it is.

- Just because there is snow on the roof doesn't mean that the fire in the stove is out. Older people may be sharper than you think.

- Keep your body moving and your mind active—if you don't use it, you lose it.

- Know your history, but avoid being stuck there.

- Life is simpler when you plow around the stump.

- Listen to the laughter of children, and remember when you were a kid.

- Might as well relax about aging—we don't have much of a choice.

- Much of growing older is a mix of holding on and letting go.

- Often we live half of our lives before we've figured out what life is.

- One of the most important things we can learn is how to get out of our own way.

- Over the hill isn't a bad thing. Climbing to the top is often difficult, coming back down not so much.

- Remember when work was fun?

- Remove the word *can't* from your vocabulary.

- Take time to write down some of your stories, tales of your childhood, your first job, your first love, turning points in your life, people who helped you along the way. You'll enjoy the activity—and so will your friends and relatives as they read your stories.

Taking Life As It Comes

- The best thing about old age is it takes a long time to arrive.

- The older the musician, the sweeter the song.

- The older you get, the less peer pressure is a problem.

- Those who have a fifth on the Fourth have trouble going forth on the fifth.

- When it comes right down to it, only a few things are important.

- Write down all your experiences, even when you don't have any.

- You know you are growing older when you visit a museum and the display includes items that were common when you were a kid.

- Maintain a sense of cheerfulness even when sadness surrounds you.

- If you go out on a limb, make sure no one nearby has a saw.

11

Conundrums and Other Wise Bits

When something sounded a little strange and difficult to figure out, my mother would say, "It's a conundrum." Today, some people would call these paradoxes. Conundrum has a better sound to it. My mother was 100 percent German, and she often used the following phrase, which to me is the ultimate conundrum: "Let's all stick together; everybody for himself." Some other conundrums I've heard along the way:

- Our strength can be our weakness; our weakness is often our strength.

- Doing less can mean doing more.

- Not knowing can be the highest level of knowledge.

- The longest road somewhere can be the shortest distance.

- That which is most hidden from us is often most present.

- Sometimes the harder we think about something, the less we understand it.

- Staying behind is sometimes the best way to get ahead.

- The greatest light can come from darkness.

- First things first, but not necessarily in that order.

- When I accept myself as I am, then I can change.

- When you give it all up, then you can have it all.

- Rather than "either...or," much of life is "both...and."

- One often misses pleasure by seeking it.

- If you must brag, do it humbly.

- People are often succeeding when they think they are failing.

- To become full, you may need to first become empty.

- The brighter you shine your light; the dimmer becomes your lantern.

- Taking charge often means letting go.

- Sometimes the harder you look the less you see.

- To know what you believe, you must know what you don't believe.

- When you come to a fork in the road, take it.

- When I am alone, I prefer to be by myself.

- If bigger is better, why is a dime worth more than a nickel?

- There are those who have nothing to do, but do it exceeding well.

Your Surroundings

I heard most of the following bits of wisdom from my dad at one time or another. He felt pretty strongly about all of them and reminded me of them often.

- Paint your house, barn, and outbuildings regularly. Keep everything around your buildings neat and tidy. Your farmstead is a window on who you are and what you value.

- Plant a few trees every year, even if you know they may never provide shade or firewood for you. There are always children and grandchildren to enjoy them—if not yours, someone else's.

- Consider carefully before cutting a tree someone says is in the way. It takes a hundred years to grow a tree and but fifteen minutes to saw it down.

- Remember that the land comes first. We must learn to listen to it and take care of it.

- To value the land and the natural world demands an appreciation that goes deeper than knowing, deeper even than understanding—to a level that involves not only the head but also the heart.

- Enjoying a rainbow usually requires experiencing a storm.

Country Roads

- For many trips, the first step is the most difficult; but no matter how long the trip, it always begins with a first step.

- The shortest distance between two points is often not the point.

- Some trips are two steps forward and one back. Better this arrangement than the opposite.

- The size of the cloud of dust tells us little about the traveler.

- It is better to be making dust than traveling in the dust that someone else has made.

- We are often so intent on our destination that we overlook the beauty along the way.

- There is probably a reason that a road is less traveled. However, the less traveled road may be the one to take.

- An unpaved road is a thing of beauty, until the dust sifts into your house every time a car passes.

- Some roads are made for traveling slowly, for contemplation along the way, for thinking deep thoughts. These roads slow you down and help you realize, by moving less quickly, that there is another side to life and to living.

- You can't know where you are going until you know where you are.

- If you don't know where you've been, you have difficulty knowing where you are headed.

- Some of the most difficult trips we make occur without ever leaving home.

- Crossing a border in our mind is often more difficult than crossing a border to another country.

- When we travel, we often learn more about where we live than about the place we visit.

- The road home is often the longest.

- It is usually a rough and crooked road to the top of the hill.

- The road down a hill is often as difficult as the road up.

- Two ways to fail: not starting, and quitting early.

- Those who promise everything usually fulfill nothing.

- It's usually a rough road to greatness.

- If you are not sure about where you are going, any road will do.

- Those who stay in the middle of the road are run over from traffic in both directions.

- Sometimes what appears as the end of the road is really only a bend.

- The joy of traveling the same road over and over again is the strong possibility of seeing something new each time.

- The journey is too long when there is no friend at the end of the trip.

- There are no shortcuts to important places.

- Every path has a few puddles.

- In any journey, it's important to stop from time to time and be thankful for the distance you have traveled.

- Some bridges should be crossed before you get to them.

- Fellow on a neighboring farm said he could run so fast that he got to where he was going before he left.

When Traveling Country Roads, Look For:

- The spires of country churches, often the highest points in the countryside. In the minds of many, they point the way to God.

- Closed country schools, some of them now homes that dotted the heartland countryside by the thousands until they were closed in the name of educational reform and better educational opportunities for country children.

- Abandoned cheese factories, located where dairy cattle were raised and milk produced. They were close enough together so farmers could haul their milk to the cheese factory with their teams and still get home in time to do a day's work on the farm.

- Clumps of lilac bushes, standing alone alongside the road. Generally they were part of a farmstead, now bulldozed over as farms grew larger and farm buildings got in the way of "progress." But the lilacs remained as silent reminders of an earlier day, when the farm family looked forward to the sweet-smelling lavender flowers each spring.

Rural Wit and Wisdom

12

Country Phrases

Rural folks in the heartland have many sayings that they commonly use. These phrases become shortcuts for communication and a way of sharing an idea without using a lot of words. But for someone from outside the region, the response to what is thought a common phrase may be "Huh?" Here are a few phrases that I grew up with and still use on occasion:

- *A pig in a poke.* Accepting something without checking it out. (A poke is a small bag.) "Jake bought the old Anderson farm; it was a pig in a poke."

- *A stone's throw away.* A short distance. "The next town is only a stone's throw away."

- *Acts like she owns the place.* A farm animal that bullies other animals. A person who acts in a high-and-mighty manner. "Janice struts around like she owns the place."

- *Afoot or horseback.* Description of a confused person. "Joe doesn't seem to know if he's afoot or horseback, the way he acts these days."

- *All worked up.* Agitated. "Jane was all worked up when she found out she was not elected president of the women's club."

- *An ax to grind.* Someone unhappy about something who makes a considerable fuss about it. Someone with an agenda. "That Billy Swensen sure has an ax to grind about the last election."

- *As easy as pie.* Not difficult to do. "Building a bird house is easy as pie."

- *Barking up the wrong tree.* Not thinking correctly about something. "Old Matt Carlson is sure barking up the wrong tree by supporting that blowhard running for Congress."

- *Bat out of hell.* Great speed. "You see Wally coming down the road? He's going like a bat out of hell."

- *Bats in the belfry.* Eccentric. Someone who does things erratically. "The way Mable's been acting lately, she must have bats in her belfry."

- *Beating around the bush.* Not getting to the point. "Listen to Adolph Sorensen; he does a lot of beating around the bush before he gets down to what he wants to say."

- *Befuddled.* Confused. "Nobody is more befuddled these days than Emory Watson—just can't tell what he's up to."

- *Better to wear out than rust out.* No matter what your age, stay active. Keep both your body and your mind working.

- *Black as the ace of spades.* Quite dark. "That October night was black as the ace of spades."

- *Blind as a bat.* When someone overlooks what seems to be obvious. "There it is, right in front of him. Oscar must be blind as a bat to not see it."

- *Brand new.* Never before used. "Just bought a brand new garden hoe."

- *Bury the hatchet.* Call a truce. Quit arguing. Settle your differences.

- *Can't cut the mustard.* Not up to the job at hand. "That kid we just hired to hoe cucumbers can't cut the mustard."

- *Cat's meow.* Something quite special. "Since Eleanor won first place with her pie at the county fair, she thinks she's the cat's meow."

- *Cat's pajamas.* Persons who believe they are better than others. "That fellow who just moved onto the old Emory place thinks he's the cat's pajamas."

- *Caught with his pants down.* When someone's position or perspective is revealed prematurely.

- *Chip off the old block.* Children who resemble their parents. "That Amy Noble acts just like her mother; she sure is a chip off the old block."

- *Clean as a whistle.* Very clean. "John finally swept out his garage. It's clean as a whistle."

- *Clear as a bell.* A sound easily heard. "You could hear Jim whistling clear as a bell."

- *Close the door; you'd think you were raised in a barn.*

- *Close your barn door.* Zip up your pants.

Rural Wit and Wisdom

- *Cobbled up.* Not put together with care. "Jeff cobbled up a new shelter for his stove wood; thing will fall down with the first heavy snow."

- *Come hell or high water.* No matter what happens.

- *Comical.* When something unexpected occurs. It may or may not be humorous. "I tell you it was comical when the back wheel fell off Fred's tractor."

- *Cool as a cucumber.* Not becoming excited or anxious about something or someone.

- *Cost an arm and a leg.* Expensive. "Joe's new tractor must have cost an arm and a leg."

- *Cracking the whip.* Being in charge and making sure things happen.

- *Crow.* Brag. "Can't hardly talk to Fred these days—all he does is crow about how good his corn is this year."

- *Dead as a doornail.* Quite dead. "Nancy bought a fancy new shade tree a few weeks ago. It's dead as a doornail."

- *Dicker.* Negotiate. "Try to buy something from Steve and all you'll do is dicker."

- *Dish to pass.* Food brought to a potluck meal. Usually a casserole. "Bring a dish to pass for the church social."

- *Doesn't have a leg to stand on.* A position that can't be defended. "Mildred doesn't have a leg to stand on—best you can say, it's her opinion."

- *Doesn't have a prayer.* Chances of being successful are slim. "Otto doesn't have a prayer in getting his grain threshed before it rains."

- *Doesn't know beans when the bag is open.* Someone who doesn't understand what is going on. "That new hired man is so dim he doesn't know beans when the bag is open."

- *Doesn't say aye, yes, or no.* When a person is asked a question and doesn't respond. "Ask the new guy at the feed store something and he doesn't say aye, yes, or no."

- *Dog tired.* Exhausted. "Hoe beans all day and you'll be dog tired."

- *Don't beat around the bush.* Get to the point.

- *Don't bet the farm on it.* Considerably risky situation.

- *Don't fuss.* Said to a host when you accept an invitation.

- *Don't hold a candle.* Inferior to what it is compared. "Did you see Nancy's dill pickles at the festival? They don't hold a candle to Jill's."

- *Don't make waves.* See *Don't muddy the water*

- *Don't muddy the water.* When things are going okay, leave them alone.

- *Don't put the cart before the horse.* First things first.

- *Down-and-out.* Very poor. "That York family is sure down-and-out."

- *Dumb cluck.* Not too bright.

- *Dumber than a stump.* A bit lacking in smarts.

- *Eats like a hog.* Better than average appetite.

- *Fast as a deer.* Someone who runs quickly.

- *Flat as a pancake.* About as flat as one can make it.

- *Fleshy.* Term used to describe an overweight person. "Did you notice that Florence has gotten a little fleshy?"

- *Flew the coop.* Left without telling anyone. "You hear about Fred's hired girl? Well, she flew the coop last night."

- *Full of wind.* Description of a person prone to exaggeration. "We pretty much agree that old Wilbur is full of wind."

- *Get down to brass tacks.* Leaving behind the extraneous and moving to the core of a problem. Dealing with basic facts.

- *Getting to the nub.* Moving to what is important. "Joe's got a way to get to the nub of the problem faster than anyone I know."

- *Going to hell in a handbasket.* Things are not going well.

- *Gone haywire.* Broken. "I don't know what we'll do; the old pump engine has gone haywire again."

- *Great weather for ducks.* Rainy.

- *Hammered.* Had too much to drink.

- *Hard row to hoe.* A difficult task. "Jill's got a hard row to hoe with that new boss she's got."

- *Having a bird.* Being agitated about something.

- *Haywire together.* To fix something temporarily. "Tell you what—I think I can haywire together that old rake and make it work one more year."

- *Head over teakettle.* Falling down, usually headfirst.

- *Healthy as an ox.* Never sick. "Fred's coming on eighty years old, and he's still healthy as an ox."

- *Hemming and hawing.* Not able to make up one's mind. "That fellow running for a spot on the county board is just hemming and hawing so as nobody has a clue what he stands for."

- *High-and-mighty.* Persons with excessive opinions of themselves.

- *High on the hog.* Living at a level beyond your neighbors.

- *High-water pants.* Trousers that you've outgrown.

- *Hit the nail on the head.* To do something properly. "You hear what Emily just said? Well she hit the nail on the head."

- *Hold down the fort.* "Take care of things while I'm away."

- *Hold your horses.* "Wait a minute; don't be so impatient."

- *Homely as sin.* Not very attractive.

- *Horse of a different color.* Someone with a different perspective. Facing a situation different from what was expected.

- *Hound-dog look.* Not very cheerful.

- *If it ain't broke, don't fix it.* Learn to leave things that work alone, whether it is a machine, some government agency, or the relationship you have with your spouse.

- *In a fix.* See *In a pickle*

- *In a pickle.* Finding oneself in a difficult situation. "Clarence was driving his old tractor up that steep hill back of his barn, and before he got halfway up he was in a pickle."

- *In the sticks.* In a rural area and quite isolated. "Joe's central Wisconsin cabin is in the sticks."

- *Isn't that just the way things go?* Sometimes things happen, and we have no control over whether they do or don't.

- *It's a doozy.* Something quite unusual. "You see that new sport coat Amos wore to church on Sunday? Well, it's a doozy."

- *It's water over the dam.* What's past is past. Forget about it.

- *Just skin and bones.* A very thin person or animal. "You'd think John would feed his old horse a little more. The critter is just skin and bones."

- *Keep your hat on.* Wait. Your time will come.

- *Keep your shirt on.* Be patient. Slow down.

- *Kit and caboodle.* An entire collection of things. "What will you take for the whole kit and caboodle?"

- *Knows the ropes.* Acquainted with the task at hand. "That new hired man sure knows the ropes when it comes to driving a tractor."

- *Knows the score.* Someone knowledgeable about what is going on.

- *Leaving behind neither hide nor hair.* Someone has disappeared without a trace. "Old Henry left without leaving behind neither hide nor hair."

- *Left holding the bag.* An unpleasant result from a negotiation or bargain. Taking the blame while others get off.

- *Let the cat out of the bag.* To reveal a secret.

- *Let the dust settle.* When matters become tense, wait a bit before moving forward.

- *Lickety-split.* Moving quickly.

- *Life of Riley.* Living the good life with few problems or concerns.

- *Like a chicken with its head cut off.* Running around with no apparent direction.

- *Living a dog's life.* Unhappy home situation.

- *Lock, stock, and barrel.* Everything. The whole thing. Phrase comes from the parts of a musket (pioneer weapon).

- *Lose your shirt.* What happens when you participate in a losing proposition.

- *Low as a snake's belly.* Not feeling good about oneself. "Since I lost my job, I feel as low as a snake's belly."

- *Make a stink.* Using harsh words to disagree with something that has happened.

- *Make hay while the sun shines.* Finish a job while the conditions are good. Never can tell when it will rain.

- *Making a beeline.* Moving straight toward some goal.

- *Making do.* Getting the job done with the resources at hand, even though they may be limited. "Henry's got the poorest old sandy farm, but he and his family are making do."

- *Mend your fences.* Restore good relations with someone.

- *Money down the drain.* Wasting resources.

- *Nailed down.* Seeing through a difficult situation, or solving a challenging problem.

- *Neck of the woods.* Referring to a specific geographic location.

- *No spring chicken.* Not so young anymore.

- *Nose to the grindstone.* Continuing to work at a difficult job without a vacation.

- *Off his feed.* Person is not feeling well and has no appetite.

- *Off the beaten path.* In an unexpected place.

- *Oh, shoot!* A very polite exclamation when something goes wrong. "'Oh, shoot!' John said when he hit his thumb with his hammer."

- *Old as dirt.* Old.

- *Older than the hills.* Quite old, but not as old as dirt.

- *On a high horse.* The person is acting superior.

- *On the fritz.* Broken. "My old pickup is on the fritz again."

- *On the mend.* When a person or an animal that has been sick is recovering.

- *One-horse town.* A rather small place.

- *Over the hill.* Too old to make a difference.

- *Pass the buck.* Shove the blame for something gone wrong onto someone else.

- *Petered out.* Quit a job before it is finished. "About three this afternoon my old Farmall tractor just petered out."

- *Pickled.* Someone who has spent too much time in a tavern.

- *Played out.* Exhausted.

- *Plowed that ground before.* Going over the same topic yet one more time.

- *Plowing along.* Continuing to do one's work.

- *Pouring money down a rat hole.* Making poor investment choices.

- *Pull someone's leg.* To kid or fool someone.

- *Put in your two cents' worth.* Adding an additional comment.

- *Put the lid on.* Stop talking.

- *Putting on the dog.* Showing off.

- *Raining pitchforks and hammer handles.* Raining hard.

- *Real McCoy.* Authentic.

- *Rocking the boat.* Disrupting an otherwise tranquil situation.

- *Ruffle some feathers.* To upset someone.

- *Rule the roost.* In charge.

- *Run like the wind.* Fast.

- *Run of the mill.* Ordinary. "Oscar's chickens are nothing fancy, just run of the mill."

- *Run out of gas.* When all of your energy is used up.

- *Runs off at the mouth.* Talks too much.

- *Scarcer than hen's teeth.* In short supply.

- *Scraping the bottom of the barrel.* Whatever it is, it's about used up.

- *Shoot off one's mouth.* Speaking without thinking.

- *Shoot the bull.* Carrying on a conversation for the sake of carrying on a conversation.

- *Short a few rungs on the ladder.* A bit slow in comprehending.

- *Short end of the stick.* Not receiving what you believe you deserve.

- *Sitting duck.* Open to criticism. Unaware of consequences.

- *Skating on thin ice.* Presenting a weak argument. Risky situation.

- *Skinny as a rail.* Quite thin. "Jake is skinny as a rail. Thinnest guy in the neighborhood."

- *Slow as molasses in January.* Not moving quickly.

- *So thin he doesn't cast a shadow.* Very skinny.

- *So tight he squeaks.* Extremely frugal. "Jesse would never buy something like that. He's so tight he squeaks."

- *Son of a gun.* Words to express surprise about something or someone. Often used when more profane words would not be appropriate.

- *Spilling the beans.* Letting someone know a previous secret. "Watch out if you tell Ethyl something; she's known for spilling the beans."

- *Spreads it on thick.* Exaggerates.

- *Straight with the world.* Lining things up so they point either north–south or east–west.

- *Strong as an ox.* Above-average strength. "That Anderson kid is strong as an ox."

- *Stumped.* Baffled by something.

- *Tail between one's legs.* Leaving a situation in disgrace.

- *Take the bull by the horns.* Taking charge of a situation.

- *Takes the cake.* When something unusual happens. "Joe won first prize with his old skinny bull at the county fair. That sure takes the cake."

- *Tall drink of water.* A tall person.

- *The babe is born.* A difficult task is completed.

- *The whole shebang.* Everything. All of it.

- *There is more than one way to skin a cat.* Most things can be accomplished in several ways. "If at first you don't succeed, just remember: there is more than one way to skin a cat."

- *Too big for one's britches.* Feeling self-important.

- *Tough as nails.* Resilient. Able to face difficult situations.

- *Tuckered out.* Exhausted. "I rowed my old leaky boat for an hour, and I'm tuckered out."

- *Turn over a new leaf.* Try to act in a different way.

- *Two shakes of a lamb's tail.* A short period of time.

- *Under the weather.* Not feeling well.

- *Until hell freezes over.* A long time.

- *Until the cows come home.* Something that takes a long time to happen.

- *Up a tree.* Caught in an unexpected situation.

- *When the horse dies, it's time to climb off.* The issue has been resolved; best to move on to something else.

- *Whistle another tune.* Coming up with another perspective, often the opposite of a previous one.

- *Windy.* Term used to describe someone who stretches the truth.

- *Worn to a frazzle.* Tired.

- *You can lead a horse to water, but you can't make it drink.* Providing an opportunity may not mean a person will take advantage of it.

13

Lifetime Learning

We must all continue learning throughout our lives, and rural people have long known the importance of doing so. Every new piece of machinery, every new crop variety, every planting season requires new learning. Stories abound about farmers who bought their first tractors after driving horses for years. To stop a horse you say whoa. Most of the time the horse will stop. Yelling whoa to a tractor is akin to yelling stop when the wind blows: nothing happens. The tractor smashes through the new tractor shed. Learning to operate a tractor thus required some unlearning, as well as some new learning.

One-Room Country Schools

Old-timers remember their days attending one-room country schools, with all eight grades in one room with one teacher. Students learned the three R's, reading, 'riting, and 'rithmetic, and they learned much more. They learned spelling, geography, and history; they learned music and art. And, above all, they learned how to learn by themselves, for the teacher usually had her hands full with a room of students at various levels of learning.

Some other things learned in a one-room country school:

- If you misbehaved at school and were punished, your punishment was likely greater when you got home.

- One of the best ways to learn is to teach someone else what you know. At the country school, older students helped younger students who may have had difficulties with one subject or another.

- Cooperation is often a better way of learning than competition. The country school was a model for cooperation.

- The country school was like a family, with the teacher as the head.

- Respect books. The one-room school library often had a limited number of them.

- Recess games such as pom-pom pull away and anti-I-over were not only fun, but they taught children of all ages how to play together and have fun doing it.

- For a country school to succeed, everyone had to help with the various duties necessary to keep the school operating—carrying in wood and water, keeping the wood-burning stove going, sweeping out the outdoor privies, putting up the flag, and keeping the schoolhouse clean and tidy.

Learning

- What we already know can prevent us from learning something new. We must first learn how to rid ourselves of old ideas and ways of doing things. We must also develop the wisdom to know what of the old to keep, for old ideas and old ways may be better than those that are new.

- Understand as much as you can about as many things as you are able, but realize that there are mysteries that cannot be understood— why a prizewinning cow dies unexpectedly, or why some summers it rains and the crops grow thick and tall, and other summers it is so dry the cows must be fed hay by mid-July.

- What we have learned is ours; no one can take it away from us.

- Our learning is sometimes hindered by our need and ability to take things apart and name each piece. By looking at pieces, we often cannot see wholes. The whole of something is usually more than the sum of its parts. A tree is more than a trunk, branches, roots, and leaves.

- We are often obsessed with accumulating answers for which there are no questions.

- Find those who are wise and follow them.

- Learn from many, be taught by all.

- Knowing is more than collecting information. Many people are informed, few know.

- We can learn from a book or another person or by doing something by ourselves. All are important, but perhaps the most important of all is learning by doing.

- Pay attention to what other people know and proclaim, but always remember that you have the right and the responsibility to develop your own perspective, your own way of thinking about and reacting to something.

- Be careful of people who seem to have all the answers—professors, preachers, politicians, and relatives. Listen politely, but then make up your own mind.

- Learn to figure in your head. You will often have the answer before someone with a fancy figuring machine.

- The world is full of people who can find fault with ideas. Those who create new ideas are few in number.

- You can learn in many ways: working at a job you don't know how to do, talking with a person you've just met, traveling to a place you've never been, eating a food you've never tasted, or walking a trail you've never hiked.

- Never stop reading. Read books, all kinds of books, fact and fiction, poetry and history, usual and unusual, and ordinary books written by local people with a story to tell and a message to share.

- Books do not scold when you blunder, laugh when you are ignorant, or hide when you seek them.

- We learn much when we least expect to: the loss of a favorite pet, the death of a person, the destruction of the corn crop when a hailstorm comes roaring through our neighborhood, the birth of a child.

- A rope is weakest at the place it is knotted. Our lives, too, are most vulnerable at the place of the knots—our unchanging perspectives, our rigid beliefs, our outdated approaches. It is when we untie our knots that we can become strong again. Untying a knot is an important form of learning.

- "What will other people think?" prevents many of us from following our interests, exploring our dreams, learning what we want most to learn, or even considering learning.

- Our teachers are many if we will recognize them as such: our children and their questions, a thunderstorm and its power, a flock of geese and their cooperation, a soaring eagle and its freedom, the promise that comes with spring, and the love between a baby and its mother.

- Learning usually takes time. If we try to learn too quickly, we will often miss the understanding that time and contemplation provide.

- Of our many loves, love for learning should be close to the top of the list.

- For each person, there is a right time for learning something and a wrong time. For instance, learning about how to operate a computer when one doesn't have a computer makes little sense.

- One of the most important things to learn is how to rid your mind of that which is not true.

- Teachers can help us learn; but we must also learn to teach ourselves.

- At the end of each day, if you have learned one new thing, consider it a good day.

- Accumulating facts and information is not learning; these are only the building blocks that may or may not contribute to learning.

- Sometimes we learn more by asking the right question than finding the answer to it.

- The most important thing we learn today may be that what we learned yesterday was wrong.

- Learning is much more than remembering. Remembering something is only the first step toward learning, the beginning of a path toward knowing.

- Be careful of too much testing and measuring, as if this were the only way to determine if learning has occurred. Many important things learned cannot be measured. How do you measure a person's reaction to a sunset? The emotional response to a poem? The development of the skills to learn on one's own and the excitement in doing it?

Teaching

Somehow, many people have gotten the idea that teaching ought be left to the professional teachers, that the rest of us have no responsibility to teach. Rural people have long known the fallacy of this position. Of course, professional teachers must be supported and applauded for their efforts, but everyone else can teach as well. Some of the teaching is direct—showing someone how to do something, such as changing the spark plugs in your tractor. Other teaching is more subtle and more often than not done by example: how we care for animals, or what we do to preserve an old barn.

- We teach by who we are and what we do, much more so than by what we say.

- Teaching is sharing and caring, listening and watching, questioning and answering, receiving and giving.

- A good teacher is one who helps students become their own teachers.

- To learn a subject well, teach it to someone else.

- Teaching involves more than facts and figures, dates and places, people and their accomplishments. Good teaching involves values and beliefs, often embedded in a tone of voice, an encouraging word, a subtle suggestion, a question raised.

- Telling a story can be a powerful way of teaching, for in a story not only the details of a matter are shared, but the opportunity is there for students to feel some of the emotion that is usually part of a story.

- Classrooms are everywhere, not merely rooms with four walls and desks in rows. Good teachers know this well. The rural countryside is a classroom without comparison.

- Good teachers create a learning environment where people are comfortable both physically and emotionally.

New and Old Ideas

Never in our history have we had so many new and old ideas colliding with each other. It seems nearly every day some new electronic device appears on the market along with advertising telling us to leave the old behind and join the march into the future with the new. We hear about new views on politics, new ideas about religion and education, we hear about climate change and endangered plant and animal species, we learn about new farming approaches, new laboratory-created seeds—the world is filled with new ideas. But what about the old ideas? Are some of them worth keeping? And how do we decide what of the old to keep and what of the new to embrace?

- Take some time to figure out what of the old you want to keep and what new ideas you want to follow. Caring about people is an old idea; buying a fancy new diesel tractor is a new idea.

- Do not equate *new* with *big*. Many people have confused these words. Avoid mixing up *big* with *better*, and, likewise, *new* with *better*. Big is often worse. So is new.

- What is worth more: a new idea or many repetitions of an old idea?

- New ideas often emerge from old ideas by giving them a new twist. The upright silo resulted when someone decided to stand a horizontal silo on end.

- Avoid making fun of your neighbor who tries something new: a new variety of corn, a different way of making hay, a new kind of wire fence, a new use for a computer. You will avoid embarrassing yourself when you discover the neighbor has something you'd like to try.

- Avoid criticizing your neighbor who insists on doing things the old way. New ways are not always better ways.

- To walk eighty rods on a never-before-traveled road is far more difficult than traveling five miles on a well-used road.

- Any new idea is suspect and subject to ridicule. New ideas are like tiny oaks; they need time to become established and push forth their leaves. Like the tiny oak, new ideas are often chewed off or smashed flat before they are recognized for what they are.

- Support a person with a new idea. It may appear foolish or unworkable, different from anything you've heard before. Give it a chance. If we never accepted a new idea, we'd still be living in caves, looking forward to the discovery of fire.

- Be careful before tossing an old idea aside—especially if the old idea involves values and beliefs, such as accepting those different from us, caring for the needy, and loving the land.

Thinking

Time for thinking is in short supply these days as people rush from one task to another, scarcely finishing one task—or even worse, working at several tasks at the same time—without taking time for a deep breath. Thinking is left for the spare moments, increasingly fewer of them, between tasks.

On the farm where I grew up, I had lots of time for thinking, as many of the tasks took a considerable amount of time to do, yet required little thinking once they were mastered. Milking cows by hand, hoeing potatoes, splitting wood, bunching freshly cut hay, and a host of similar tasks. I could work at the task, indeed, do it well, and at the same time allow my mind to wander onto all sorts of topics, both large and small—a news report I'd recently read in the paper, a comment another farmer made at the mill while I waited with Pa to have our grist ground into cow feed, or something our teacher said in school that got me looking at something in a new way.

Country people value time for thinking and know the importance of it. They also know the dangers of allowing others to do their thinking for them; for instance, buying into an ideology that sounds good on the surface, but is deeply flawed when thought about carefully. Country people take time to think—most of them, anyway.

- If you do not think for yourself, you do not think at all.

- We are all entitled to our own thoughts. So are other people entitled to their thoughts.

- There is a time for thinking and a time for action.

- We become what we think.

- If we all thought alike, what a boring world it would be.

- Before knowing comes thinking.

- Learning how to think may be the most important thing we learn in life.

- Once you've lost control of your thoughts, you've lost control of your actions.

- As your thinking changes, so do your actions.

- Thinking before speaking is a difficult lesson for many people to learn.

- When in doubt, stop and think.

- There is a difference between thinking and rearranging your opinions.

- Discarding an old way of thinking can be one of the most difficult things we do.

- Clear thinking can result in a changed mind. A changed mind can result in a new approach to facing the world.

- Working with your hands can often unsnarl difficult thoughts.

- We can never lose our freedom to think.

Thinking and Doing

Thinking and doing go together; especially is that so with farm work. Thinking about what you are doing almost always makes the task easier, safer, and more satisfying.

- Take time to think in the middle of doing. A few minutes thinking can save hours of doing.

- Doing without thinking is dangerous; thinking without doing is misguided.

- Sometimes we must do and think at the same time.

- Avoid doing too much thinking about a task before starting to do it.

- To be caught thinking while not doing is to be labeled lazy. The answer: keep doing.

Learning from Everyday Things

14

We often overlook the opportunity to learn from the everyday things in our lives, which we encounter regularly and often take for granted. Rural people have long known that learning can occur from the most ordinary of things and in the most common situations. A key to this learning is not facing ordinary tasks as another kind of drudgery to be endured, but as an opportunity for gaining some new insight, some new way of thinking, some unique window on the world. We ignore our surroundings because they are so common. We don't bother to look at our old barn, which may be a hundred years old and a thing of beauty, or the white oak tree that shades our farm home, or the country road that snakes by our place, and much more. Rural people have long known

that with a bit of thought, even the most ordinary can be quite extraordinary. Here are a few examples I have discovered along the way.

Firewood

People who cook their food and heat their homes with woodstoves spend a considerable amount of time each year, usually in the fall, making wood. Making wood includes several tasks: cutting trees (usually those that are dead or dying), slicing the wood into blocks that are then split into sizes that will fit in the woodstoves, and, finally, stacking the wood, preferably in a woodshed or other location so the wood is out of the weather. Some things learned from making wood:

- Those who cut their own wood are several

times warmed before the wood ever is pushed into the woodstove.

- Every tree has its own way of growing, and thus it requires some thinking about how to avoid being injured when cutting it down.

- Keep your ax and crosscut saws sharp. A sharp tool helps prevent injury and makes the cutting much easier.

- There is a right way to use an ax and a crosscut saw, which is true of every tool.

- Each axman must discover his own rhythm for using an ax. Once the rhythm is discovered, the work becomes much easier.

- Allow the crosscut saw to do the work—don't force it or try to make it do more than it's capable of doing.

- Master wood splitting. Discover how to read a block of wood, the direction of the grain, and the location of the knots.

- Reading a block of wood and understanding it makes the work easier, just as learning how to read another person may also help to make the relationship easier.

- Enjoy the smell of fresh-cut wood; it has a special fragrance uniquely different from the many smells in nature.

- Marvel at how a block of firewood has stored the sun's energy and releases it when the wood is burned, providing heat for your home. As a battery stores electricity, a block of wood stores heat.

- Learn to identify the difference between oak and birch, pine and cherry, and cedar and aspen by sight and smell from the blocks of wood cut from these trees.

- A properly stacked pile of wood can be a thing of beauty, with the blending of shapes and sizes, smells and colors.

- A woodpile is a symbol of achievement, a visible sign of the hard work that went into building it.

- Neighbors sometimes compete, often without comment, about the size and structure of their woodpiles. "You have a good-looking woodpile" are words of endearment for a country person.

- Learn which firewood starts burning quickly (pine and cedar) and which wood heats hottest and longest (oak, hickory, cherry, and black locust).

Trees

Most of us have associated with trees our entire lives. We've climbed in them as kids, enjoyed their shade on hot, sunny days, and sat under them and listened to a breeze play with the leaves. We take trees for granted until a windstorm drops one on our porch or a big tree stands in the way of an "important" building project or a new road. We too often take for granted the positive features of trees.

- To see strength and patience, observe a tree.

- A tree is a natural air conditioner.

- Few songs are more beautiful than the wind in the trees.

- Plant a tree and carve out a piece of the future.

- Truly remarkable persons are those who plant trees knowing full well they will never enjoy the shade.

- You are never too old to plant a tree.

- A tree knows enough to rest during part of the year.

- Does anyone see the contradiction of cutting down all the trees in a development and then naming the streets after them?

- For some, a tree is a thing of beauty; for others, it is something that stands in the way of progress.

- Think about all the history a hundred-year-old tree has experienced—and yet it still grows, uncomplaining, providing shelter for wild creatures and shade for one who travels by.

- Can you imagine that when you carry a pocketful of acorns, you may be carrying an oak forest?

Walking

I grew up doing lots of walking. Merely doing the daily chores required plenty of it. We walked to the country school a mile away, and when we visited a close neighbor, those who were only a mile or so from our farm, we walked. On Sunday afternoons in summer, we walked around the farm, inspecting the crops, checking on how well the oats were growing,

Rural Wit and Wisdom

how well the corn was doing, and how the cow pasture was faring with the spell of dry weather we'd been having. Walking was as natural as breathing, and although as a kid I didn't think about it, I learned much from walking.

- Walking allows for thinking, for sorting out feelings and impressions, for making decisions about matters both important and not, for coming to grips with that which may have been so far elusive.

- One of the best ways to solve a problem is to walk. It may take a mile; it may take longer.

- A walk in nature always reveals more than you were looking for.

- Want to come up with something new, something special, something creative? Take a walk.

- Even if you limp, you are still walking.

- Walking not only gets the blood flowing, but it gets the brain thinking.

- The best way to cool a short temper is to take a long walk.

- In our fast-paced world, walking slows us down.

- There is no better way to learn about nature than a long walk in the outdoors.

- When we walk, we see more, hear more, smell more, feel more than when we speed through life as most of us do.

- Walking will get you much farther in life than talking.

- Walking requires one step at a time.

- One of the great achievements of life is to walk where no one else has walked before.

- We must all learn when to walk away from something.

- Some people walk too long in the same place.

- Wisdom is knowing when to follow the path that others have walked and when to make a new path.

- Walking alone can be a great pleasure; so can walking with another person.

A Rainy Day

On the sandy farm in central Wisconsin where I grew up, we almost never had enough rain for good crop production. So every rainy day was a blessing, providing not only a reprieve from farm work, but also a necessity for making a living.

- Never curse the rain; it is necessary for life to continue.

- Without a rainy day, we would have little appreciation for the sunny ones.

- No one knows you're crying when you are walking in the rain.

- Be young again; jump in a puddle.

- Without rain there would be no rainbows.

- There are those who want rain without thunder and lightning.

- Irish blessing: "May the road rise up to meet you, may the wind be ever at your back. May the sun shine warm upon your face and the rain fall softly on your fields. And until we meet again, may God hold you in the hollow of his hand."

- The best thing to do on a rainy day is to let it rain.

- Next to the top of all farmer discussion is the rain. When will it rain again? When will it stop raining?

- Sit under a pine tree on a rainy day. Listen to the message of raindrops on pine needles; it's spoken in nature's language, profound and mystical.

- Rainy days are for contemplation and philosophical thoughts.

- Delight in a rainy day. It is nature's way of cleansing and refreshing the land, and it's a time to relax from work that is now postponed.

- Enjoy a thunderstorm. Be awed at the power of lightning, and always be thankful for the rainfall. Some soil seems never to have enough.

- Climb the ladder to the haymow on a rare rainy day in July. Rest on the fresh hay, and listen to the raindrops drum on the roof overhead; it is like being inside a big drum with a mysterious force making music all around you. Smell the aroma of sweet clover and alfalfa, and feel the softness of the hay beneath you. Be thankful that you are alive, at this time and in this place.

The Wind

Although we can't see wind, we can surely see what it's capable of doing. Few invisible things have such power. I've seen the damage it can do, as well as the good. Wind can uproot trees and destroy buildings. It can ruin a dream and cool a sweaty brow. We can try to ignore it at our peril, as it comes and goes, as it has for eons and will likely do so for eons to come.

- Enjoy the wind. Embrace it. But always respect it.

- Watch the wind play with the surface of a pond, creating ripples and riffles that form and disappear. An invisible artist at work.

- Listen to the creaks and squeaks of an old windmill on a windy night in fall. Allow your mind to create fearsome unknown creatures that are battling for the rights to the night.

- Listen to the wind sift through the bare tree limbs of winter, making a lonely, sorrowful sound.

- Hear the summer wind softly caress the white pine needles, set the aspen leaves into nervous chatter, and cause the maple leaves to flutter like so many little fans.

- It is easy to move with the wind; it is moving against the wind that shows true character.

Old Barns

Some of the finest old barns in the United States are found in the heartland, especially in those regions where dairy farming was an important agricultural activity. Today, many of these barns are over a hundred years old and still standing tall—those that have been taken care of with new roofs and attention to walls. Many others are in disrepair, forgotten pieces of agricultural history pushed aside with modern advances in caring for dairy cattle.

- Barns are agricultural history in red paint, sociology with gable roofs, theology with lightning rods.

- Every barn has a story to tell—of the changing of the seasons, of the sweet smell of hay piled high in the haymows, of spring rains drumming on the roof, of cold winter winds tearing around its corners, of farmers who spent their entire lives milking cows and doing chores inside its four walls.

- A barn is like a cathedral, a vast expanse of space holding back the elements and connecting people to a larger power.

- Tear down an old barn and destroy a piece of your heritage.

- Stand inside an empty barn on a windy day; listen to it complain as the wind whistles around the corners and rattles the hinges on the doors.

- Enjoy the warmth of a cow barn on a cold day in winter. It is a natural warmth created by the animals housed there and so different from the artificial heat that warms your home.

- There is no orchestra that can surpass the sound of rain on a barn roof.

- Join a barn preservation group, and share the satisfaction that you are helping save an important piece of agricultural history.

- If it's a choice between putting a new roof on the barn or on the house, choose the barn. If your farm animals are uncomfortable, you may soon not have a barn or a house roof to replace.

The Land

We walk on it, grow things in it, destroy it with parking lots and fancy buildings, and mostly take it for granted. Seldom do we ponder the deeper meanings of land, the profound ties that all humankind has to it. Ties that are at the same time economic and spiritual, practical and lofty.

- The land is a mystery. It constantly surprises and sometimes disappoints. But it is always the land.

- Land: they are not making any more of it, so we must protect what we have.

- The land is always changing, but remains changeless.

- When we treat the land like a machine, measuring it and testing it, forming it and shaping it, it often rebels. The land is reminding us that it too lives. None of us wants to be treated like a machine. Neither does the land.

- The land is soil, but much more. Land is never dirt. Dirt is what accumulates behind the refrigerator and what we track into the kitchen on our shoes.

- When we own land, it also owns us.

- We really can't own land. We are only stewards for a time as the land moves from owner to owner.

- It is the land that is the foundation for everything. It feeds our bodies, anchors our homes, and nourishes our souls.

- A foundation for human ethics rests in our relationship to the land.

- How people care for the land today is an indicator of whether they will have food and shelter tomorrow.

- How a person treats the land is a window into how a person treats other people.

- The extent to which we sever our connections with the land is the extent to which we disconnect ourselves from our souls.

Field Stones

Our home farm was on the terminal moraine where the last great glacier stopped. The glacier left behind hills and valleys, lakes and streams, and above all it left field stones. Each spring, before the crops could be planted, the stones had to be picked, for if left, they caused great harm to our farm machinery. Picking stones was hard, dirty work, as the stones, some as big as a kitchen stove and bigger, were heavy and difficult to move. But move them we did, every year, for as my father said, "If nothing else comes up on this farm, we know the stones will." Indeed they did, as the freezing and thawing of winter brought them to the surface each year.

I despised the stones, but also respected them, and, indeed, later, saw many of their positive characteristics.

- Stones in the fields of many sizes and hues— red, brown, gray, black. In the way. Despised. Cursed.

- Stones off the fields of many shapes and colors—foundations for barns and churches, homes and schools. Useful. Beautiful. Praised.

- Working in a stony field, like life, requires you

to be constantly alert. You never know when you will come up against a hardheaded stone that you didn't see. Failing to act quickly can mean a broken plow point, a twisted cultivator shovel, or a dulled sickle bar on your mower.

- A stony field builds character—at least, it keeps you awake when you are cultivating it.

- *Carved in stone* to a farmer usually means that his broken plow point has done the deed.

- Leaving no stone unturned has a special meaning for a farmer with a stony field.

Farm Dog

Her name was Fanny. She was a Scotch collie, brown with a white mane and a long pointed nose, and she was our dog—more correctly she was Pa's dog, as he had trained her, and she was his constant companion on the farm. Farm dogs were a part of a farm family, just as the team of draft horses were. But Fanny was even more a part of our family than usual, because we depended on her to help with the work of the farm, just as Pa depended on my brothers and me to help with the farm work.

Fanny had several jobs around the farm. She kept the chicken flock away from the house, announced the arrival of any newcomer with a few loud barks, and guarded the place at night, barking loudly if some critter came too close to the house, such as a fox intent on raiding the chicken house. She accompanied us squirrel hunting and had an uncanny ability to spot a squirrel high up in an oak tree, hidden among the leaves. But perhaps most importantly, Pa had trained her to fetch the cows from the far pasture without any of us needing to accompany her. In early evening, when it was time for milking, Pa would simply say, "Fanny, go fetch the cows." She would look up at him, wag her tail a couple times, and trot off up the lane back of the barn and sometimes travel for half a mile to one of the far pastures where the cattle grazed. A short time later, we'd spot the dairy herd, all strung out in a straight line with Fanny at the very end, wagging her tail and barking occasionally if some young heifer wanted to challenge her order to keep moving down the trail toward the barn.

Once the cows were in the barnyard, waiting for one of us to open the barn door and let them inside, Fanny moved among the cattle putting her nose to a cow's nose and then moving onto another cow and repeating—a kind of dog-to-cow conversation? Certainly a sign of respect between cows and the farm dog.

- Farm dogs have their own kind of wisdom— some of it mysterious and unknown to us who watch their behavior; some of it rather obvious and something that can provide an example for our own behavior.

- Farm dogs are loyal and trustworthy, anxious to please, and always doing their work to the best of their abilities.

- Farm dogs expect little in return for their good work—something to eat, shelter from a storm, and their owner's respect.

- A farm dog, different from some people, never wavers in how she treats people. When asked to a do a job, the dog never questions, doesn't talk back, never says she won't or can't do something.

- Learn to be a partner with your dog. She excels at many things—she runs faster than you, can literally smell out problems that you can't detect, and hears sounds you can't hear.

Farmhouse

The farmhouse where I grew up was not fancy. It was two stories tall, with three large bedrooms on the second floor and two downstairs, plus a kitchen, dining room, and parlor on the downstairs floor. The basement was really a cellar with a dirt floor, with bins for potatoes and shelves for storing mother's canning.

The house, built in about 1900, was not insulated and was heated with two woodstoves: one in the kitchen (the cookstove) and a Round Oak stove in the dining room. During the late fall and winter months, one downstairs bedroom and the parlor were closed off, which meant the five of us (my mother, dad, and two brothers) lived in the two downstairs rooms. My brothers and I slept in the bedroom above the dining room, which was partially heated by the stovepipe from the dining room's woodstove. On cold winter nights, when the stove sputtered out about midnight, the house became as cold as an icehouse, especially the upstairs hall and bedroom where we slept.

The kitchen was the center of all activities in the house. It was around the kitchen table that decisions were made about farming operations. A checkered oilcloth usually covered the wooden table, and in the center stood a kerosene lamp that provided light, as we had no electricity. It was in the kitchen where we entertained visitors (except in midsummer, when Ma insisted that we sit in the parlor when city relatives visited). It was in the kitchen where we ate all our meals, except for celebrations such as Thanksgiving, Christmas, and Easter, and when the threshing crew came by and the larger dining room table was needed to seat everyone.

A wood-burning cookstove had a prominent place at the west end of the kitchen, with its seemingly always-empty wood box standing by its left side. Attached to the stove on the right side was the reservoir, providing us with warm water. Hot water was available from the ever-present teakettle that steamed through the day on the back of the stove, ready for thawing a frozen pipe or making a cup of tea.

A door just to the right of the stove opened to the woodshed, attached to the west side of the kitchen. A second door, on the south side of the kitchen, opened to the porch and then to the outside. We had a second door to the outside, from the dining room, but this was never used, except in summer to let in some cooler air.

The kitchen sink was on the north wall of the kitchen, with the old, dented water pail sitting on its edge, as we had no indoor plumbing. The icebox, an upright model with space for a fifty-pound block of ice in its upper compartment, stood to the right of the sink. The iceman came by once a week and lifted in a new block of ice, which, during the warm summer months, had shrunk to the size of a brick and sometimes even smaller. To the right of the icebox was a door leading into the pantry and from the pantry another door leading to the cellar beneath the house.

Even though the farmhouse was where our family slept and ate meals, where we did our homework and played cards, and where we entertained visitors, the house always took second place to the barn. As Pa always said, "No money comes out of the house." As a result, most improvements on the farm took place first in the barn. For example, we had running water in the barn twenty years before there was indoor plumbing in the house. The cows needed ready access to drinking water for the production of milk. My mother never questioned Pa's decisions concerning where to spend our very limited resources.

I learned several things that centered around our farmhouse.

- If animals are providing the income for the farm, then their comfort must come before that of the family, if it's necessary to make a choice.

- My mother, even though as frugal as frugal could be, insisted the parlor, with a good carpet, sofa, and matching chair, be kept in good order so the city relatives could be properly impressed when they visited during the summer months.

- A wood-burning cookstove, with a hint of oak smoke mixing with the cooking and baking, always provided a homey, comfortable atmosphere in the kitchen.

15
Getting Along

Living in the country means getting along with all kinds of folks. You never know when you might need someone to help you out. Neighbors are especially prized. When I was growing up, our neighbors represented several ethnic groups—German, Norwegian, Welsh, Bohemian, Polish, English—and an array of religious persuasions. Some were Lutheran, some Catholic, a handful were Methodists and Baptists, a few were Presbyterians, and a few more belonged to no church and were quite proud of it. Some were good farmers, several so-so, and a couple families ought to have been doing something else, but they continued to struggle along, never quite learning what farming was all about.

One family had become thieves, stealing wrenches from machinery left in the fields and committing other dishonest acts, including stealing our barn cats. My brothers, when visiting at this farm one day, spotted the cats, caught them, and took them home. "Don't steal our cats anymore," my brothers said. And they didn't. But they continued stealing other things.

Everyone in the neighborhood knew this was a family of thieves. We simply put up with it by avoiding leaving our wrenches in our machines and keeping a close eye on things around the farmstead when someone from this family came visiting. No one ever considered reporting them to the sheriff—after all, they were our neighbors.

Of course, we needed to get along with people beyond our neighborhood. It was important to be on good terms with the business people in town: the miller who ground our cow feed, the cheese maker at the local cheese factory where we sold our milk, the grocer who traded our eggs for groceries, the blacksmith who pounded out our plow points and fixed our always-breaking machinery, the banker who watched over our meager financial resources, and a host of others. We depended on them—they depended on us, too, of course.

Not everyone got along. People got into arguments with each other, often about politics, but on many other topics as well. Sometimes they wouldn't talk to each other for years. This included neighbors and former friends and especially relatives. It was hard for kids when they heard from their parents, "Oh, you can't go fishing with Johnny. We don't have anything to do with that family." You'd gotten to know Johnny in school, and he seemed to be a good guy.

Some ways for getting along:

- A promise made is a promise kept. To go back on your promise is a form of lying—an unforgiveable shortcoming.

- Consider everyone honest until they say or do something to indicate otherwise.

- Overlook bad manners, disagreeable behavior, and lack of responsiveness the first time. Everyone has a bad day.

- Nothing quells a disagreement faster than refusing to raise your voice to those who raise their voice to you.

- To shout back when you are shouted at allows the other person to take control of the interchange.

- Remember that silence is often the best answer.

- Words you are most likely to hear and remember are those spoken softly and not yelled.

- When you are furious with someone, hold your tongue. When you get home, write the person a letter, venting all your anger. Burn the letter.

- The best thing to do in many situations is nothing.

- If you can't say something good about a person, say nothing at all.

Rural Wit and Wisdom

- You cannot unsay a cruel word.

- A handshake is as good as a written contract. Easier, too, because you don't have to fish around through a cluttered bureau drawer to find a piece of paper to write a few words. Be clear on what you agree. If you have questions, ask them before you shake hands.

- If you have any doubts whatever about what you and another person are agreeing to, do get the agreement down on paper with two signatures and a date. This avoids many potential problems that may crop up later.

- Sometimes it's hard to fit in when you think you should stand out.

- What you think of me is none of my business.

- What it comes down to is that all you can be is you—and that is quite enough.

- Learn how to leave some things alone.

- Listen to the views of others, but trust your own as well.

- Some people are hard to listen to because their actions speak more loudly than their words.

- Watch out for those who use big words. In most cases, if they knew what the words meant, they wouldn't use them.

Being Yourself

- Be yourself. Don't pretend to be who you are not.

- Always striving for the approval of others is to have your compass set in the wrong direction.

- In our haste to seek approval from others, we overlook searching for approval of ourselves.

- Your reputation is what people think you are; your character is who you are.

- We all have imperfections; it's what makes us special.

- It's never too late to become what you are capable of becoming.

- One of our most challenging tasks is to come out from behind ourselves.

- Always be yourself, because the people that matter don't mind, and the ones that mind don't matter.

- If you must worry about one or the other,

worry more about your character, not your achievements.

- Some people wait to have others figure out who they are. Who you are is for you to figure out, all by yourself.

- Define yourself. It's one of the responsibilities of living.

- We gain respect by earning it.

- Remember your name; once it is tarnished, it will remain so.

- It is the outside of a person that we see, but what's inside is most important.

- As hard as we may try, no one ever fools a child.

Strangers and Salespeople

- When strangers appear at your door, invite them in and offer them a cup of coffee. Another day you may be a stranger knocking on an unknown door.

- When fixing a meal, always be prepared to set one more table place, and sometimes more than one. You just never know who might drop by, and to not offer them food if they arrive at mealtime would be rude.

- Try to be polite with your spouse's city relatives who make a habit of arriving at your house at mealtime, especially the ones with a gaggle of hungry kids.

- If you arrive at someone's house at mealtime, the polite thing to do is to accept a cup of coffee and perhaps dessert, but don't eat the entire meal.

- Urban strangers and salespeople are those who trek up to your never-used front door and search for a doorbell that is not there. Some realize, after the first embarrassing moments, that they are trying to enter where no one has entered before, and they find their way around to the kitchen door. Treat them as the strangers they are. Avoid judging them, for they know not the ways of country people.

- Be wary of the salesperson who takes too much for granted, such as the vacuum cleaner salesman who insists on spreading his little bag of dirt in the living room to demonstrate the prowess of his machine, only to discover a moment later that the farmer does not have electricity.

Marriage

Getting along usually starts at home, with dad and mother and kids getting along.

- Little things keep a marriage alive: a word of praise, an unexpected gift, a trip to town for dinner.

- Being kind is more important than being perfect.

- Hugs speak of caring. Hug your spouse. Hug your kids. Do this often.

- Trust is key in keeping a family together and a marriage alive.

- Always sit down and talk through a disagreement rather than letting it fester unresolved. But wait a little before you talk to allow the anger to disappear and the emotions to calm.

- *Love* is sometimes a hard word for many rural people to say. Spouses like to hear it from each other at least once a day, even when the excuse is "She knows it, why must I say it?"

- My wife says I never listen to her. At least, I think that's what she said.

16

Seasonal Changes

Seasonal changes dramatically influence people who live in the heartland, especially those who live in the northern states. Heartlanders enjoy each season, mostly, but always patiently anticipate the next season to come. This is especially so of winter, which is likely the most maligned and underappreciated of all the seasons. A hot summer, not uncommon, also evokes complaints and fond memories of colder weather, the same kind of weather that was criticized only a few months earlier.

Spring

In spring we shake loose the shackles of winter and make big plans and think big thoughts. We celebrate what has passed and look forward to the future with joy and hope. In no other season is there such anticipation. Spring is melting snow and mud. Mud in the road. Mud in the fields. Mud tracked into the kitchen. Spring is maple syrup and flooding streams, green grass and frisky calves, open windows and cows on pasture.

Different from summer and winter when we speak of midseasons, we do not speak of midspring, because there is no such thing. Spring comes in fits and starts, one day warm and sunny, the next day cold and snowy. And then spring disappears and we have summer. One thing does progress in spring—the amount of light each day increases as the spring days pass. A glorious contrast to the dark and gloomy days of winter.

In spring:

- Listen for meltwater dripping from a snowy roof.

- Watch for Canada geese winging north.

- Listen to pond frogs making a noisy production of spring's arrival.

- Listen for a ruffed grouse drumming on a log deep in the woods west of the cabin.

- Hear the first robin's song.

- See a pair of sandhill cranes winging overhead, calling their prehistoric calls.

- Smell bedsheets that have hung on the clothesline for a couple hours.

- Listen to the creaking of harness leather as the team of horses pulls a walking plow.

- Smell freshly turned soil after the plow has turned a furrow, a ribbon of brown across the formerly green pasture.

- Feel the sunshine on your back when you hike to the still-frozen pond.

- Smell the blossoms of wild cherry, plum, apple, and black locust.

- Feel the March wind that tears the dead oak leaves off the trees and sends dry leaves scurrying across the yard.

- Feel the first spring rain on your face.

- Watch cows kick up their heels when they are turned out to pasture for the first time after months of confinement in a barn.

- Watch newly born kittens tumble over each other in their play.

- Feel the excitement that comes with the first warm, sunny days, and learn not to despair when snowflakes and cold return, as they often do in spring.

- We need winter to truly enjoy spring.

Summer

Summer is enduring heat and hungry insects, days beginning before dawn and ending after dark, never-ending work. Summer is bluegill fishing, swimming in the pond, and watching free outdoor movies in town on Tuesday nights. Summer is often dry weather, when the sun shines day after day and the land becomes parched, when old-timers claim that during the driest years the rivers ran only on Tuesdays and Thursdays.

Summer is the hurry-up season, where there is always more work to do than time to do it. For country people, summer does not mean time for a vacation.

In summer:

- Listen to the wind blowing across a tallgrass prairie.

- Listen for the rustle of corn leaves on a quiet night in August.

- Hear the clattering of a hay mower slicing off alfalfa.

- Smell fresh-cut hay curing in the field and fresh peas cooking on a woodstove.

- Hear the sound of a steel-wheeled wagon lumbering along a country road, the steel wheels meeting gravel stones and making a grating, protesting sound.

- Enjoy the sound of a two-cylinder John Deere tractor working in the distance—*pop, pop.*

- Listen for the gentle call of a Holstein cow summoning her newborn calf.

- Enjoy the sound of bullfrogs at the pond singing slow and deep, a strange but beautifully haunting tune.

- Listen for water gurgling along a rocky stream, moving from its meager beginnings to eventually tumbling into the ocean.

- Smell horse sweat, a pungent and earthy smell.

- Smell country road dust that hangs in the air when a car passes.

- Stop and reflect on the warmth of summer as you think about the cold days of winter to come.

- Find time to go swimming in the lake where you and your brothers and the hired man swam on hot summer days when the chores were done at day's end.

- Remember the hired man's Ford Model T car—we traveled on country roads with the top down and a cloud of dust boiling up behind us, and the cool breeze of the car's movement a pleasant contrast to a hot summer evening.

- Look forward to Tuesday evenings because Tuesday night was free show night in town. The projectionist nailed a bedsheet to a two-by-four fastened to a giant black willow tree and we sat outside under the stars and watched movies and swatted mosquitoes and watched mostly Westerns with lots of horse riders chasing and shooting at each other.

- Sit under a shade tree and sip lemonade, and remember what the weather was like six months ago.

Fall

Fall means filling silo, husking corn, and gathering orange pumpkins before the first hard freeze. Fall is squirrel hunting, apple picking, and sorghum making. It is a gathering time as the crops are harvested, the cattle are herded into the barn, and the family gathers around the kitchen woodstove to eat freshly made popcorn.

Fall is harvest time, when the proof of the planting and the summer care of the crops is realized, when the hard work of spring and summer is seen with filled barns of hay, corncribs brimming with ears, granary bins running over, and the cellar under the house well stocked with potatoes, onions, rutabagas, pumpkins, and squash.

In fall:

- Listen for the sound of the school bell echoing in the valley, announcing the beginning of the fall term.

- Hear the barking of a gray squirrel on a quiet evening, just as the sun is setting.

- Listen for the hooting of an owl deep in the woods to the north, when there is no other sound.

- Hear a wild turkey gobbling, trying to impress some hens.

- Listen to the rustling of corn leaves in the shocks that march across the stubbled corn field like so many teepees.

- Hear the corn shredder shudder as cob-heavy cornstalks are pushed into the machine, and yellow corncobs tumble into the corn wagon, and crushed stalks and leaves fly out the blower pipe.

- Feel the first cold rain of the season splattering on your face as you go for the cows on a dreary October morning.

- Feel the frost underfoot when you walk to the barn for the early morning chores.

- Feel the smooth skin of a ripe red apple before biting into it.

- Smell fallen leaves on the forest floor as you search for dead oak trees to cut for the woodstove.

- Smell sorghum juice boiling in a kettle, a hint of the sweet flavor to follow when you spread the sorghum syrup on a slice of fresh bread.

- Smell homemade vegetable soup simmering on the back of the wood-burning cookstove, the aroma of soup mixing with a hint of wood smoke.

- Smell hay in the barn loft, the aroma of dried alfalfa, clover, and timothy engulfing you as you fork hay from the mow to the eagerly waiting cattle below.

- Smell newly dug potatoes piled high in the cellar under the house, a subtle earthy smell.

- Celebrate the harvest with a Thanksgiving dinner that brings the family together. Aunts, uncles, cousins, all gathered around the big dining room table that has all of its leaves added so it nearly fills the room. Enjoy roast duck and roast beef and ham, but no roast turkey, because Pa doesn't like turkey, says it's too dry and without flavor.

- Walk in the woods behind the house and smell fall everywhere—the pungent smell of fallen leaves and dead grass, the sweet smell of clear air coming from the north, coming from Canada, where winter is already beginning to settle in.

- Smell oak smoke trickling from the kitchen chimney, reminding you that Ma is probably baking apple pies from the apples you picked in the orchard yesterday.

Winter

Winter is for slowing down, a time for reflection and taking stock of the year that has passed and the year that is coming. Winter is for relaxing, for reading a good book, for putting together a puzzle, for visiting a friend, for taking a long walk. For slipping on a pair of skis and sliding across an open field. For pulling on a pair of skates and making a few turns on the frozen pond, just to prove that you can still do it.

Winter is the quiet season, when the only sounds are the wind sifting through the naked tree branches and the call of a lone crow in the woods to the north.

In winter:

- Remember it as a time for warm memories.

- Realize that winters in years past were so cold that when a man cussed, the words froze and you didn't hear them until the next spring.

- Recall that some Eskimos have fifty-two names for snow—one name seems sufficient when you have to shovel it.

- Listen for ice cracking on the pond, leaving fissures that spread across the expanse of the windswept surface. Mysterious sounds of protest.

- Enjoy the snow and feel sorry for those who live in southern climes, who can't look out the window and see the beauty of winter.

- Listen to the howl of a blizzard, which rattles the windows and piles snow high against the barn door.

- Hear the creak and squeak of snow as you walk along the road on a below-zero morning.

- Hear the crunch of snow under snowshoes when you shuffle across a snow-buried field.

- Enjoy the laughter of children as they belly flop on their sleds and race down the long hill back of the schoolhouse.

- Listen to the crackling of wood burning in the woodstove and the gentle sound of steam rising from the teakettle.

- Feel the warmth of your favorite cap and the comfort of your leather mittens, with their home-knitted wool liners that have served you well for many winters.

- Look for the Big Dipper hanging in the northern sky on a clear, crisp, snowy night. Wonder about the millions of stars that surround you and where they came from, and, at the same time, wonder about where you came from.

- Learn to find the North Star, pointed to by the upper right star of the Big Dipper and high in the northern sky. If you can find the North Star, even if you are lost, you at least know your directions.

- Be amazed by the northern lights when they appear across the northern horizon, as they often do in late fall and winter. Beginning as a glow, they become an extravaganza of shifting shafts of light and multiple colors, constantly changing and always special.

- Stand in a snowstorm and allow the snowflakes to pellet your face. Feel the power of the wind and the challenge of the cold. Recall the days when you walked a mile to school in a snowstorm and all you could think of as you walked was the warmth of the schoolroom, a long way ahead of you on the country road.

- Go ice fishing. Sit by a smoky fire and listen to your father and uncles swap stories about the big fish they've caught in the past, fish that gain weight and length with each telling of the story.

- Don't make too small a hole in the ice when ice fishing. Nothing is more embarrassing or perplexing than hooking a fish too large for the hole. Same with life. Be prepared for the big opportunities; they often come along when you least expect them.

- Remember, no matter what direction a north wind blows, it always blows cold.

- Read a good book—a book you have meant to read for some time and put off. An opportunity to read the classics like *The Grapes of Wrath*, *The Old Man and the Sea*, *The Great Gatsby*, *A Sand County Almanac*, and *Walden*. A time to become reacquainted with John Steinbeck, Ernest Hemingway, F. Scott Fitzgerald, Aldo Leopold, and Henry David Thoreau, and perhaps a few more, such as John Muir, Sigurd Olson, and Edwin Way Teale. Time to read a book of poetry and appreciate the poet's lean use of words, making every word count. Try

Carl Sandburg, Robert Frost, or Walt Whitman's *Leaves of Grass*, and then go on from there.

- Listen for the silence of winter, when the snow buries the land and cold tightens its grip, turning breath into clouds and thickening the ice on the lakes. There is great beauty in silence, something that we have little of these days.

- Hike in the woods on a below-zero morning and listen and hear nothing except your heart beating.

- On January 1, put a smile on your face and a spring in your step, and forget last year's mistakes.

- Remember that the best thing you can do when it is snowing is to let it snow.

17

One with Nature

Living in the country means living close to nature. Seeing wild animals is an everyday occurrence, whether it is a whitetail deer standing in the field just outside the kitchen window, or a turkey gobbler strutting along the trail leading up the hill beyond the barn. Occasionally, nature comes a little too close for even a country person. One of those times is when a skunk builds a den under the porch or a groundhog decides to burrow under the wall in the shed. Another uncomfortable situation is when a furry brown bat takes up residence in your attic and on a warm summer evening wakes you up when it swoops around your bedroom, lost on its way to the outside.

Nature also comes too close when a deer sneaks into your vegetable garden and destroys an entire row of peas plus most of a row of green beans in one night. And then, a few weeks later, a raccoon, wearing its black mask, emerges from the woods, steals into your garden, and ruins fifteen ears of new sweet corn.

But these are the exceptions, the low points in nature-human interactions. Most of the time the relationships are congenial, wild animals and humans living together, not excessively disrupting each other's lives. Of course, nature is more than deer, skunks, bats, and raccoons. And there is much more to a relationship with nature than encounters with wild animals.

- Our spirits are connected to nature—to the whip-poor-will's call in spring, to the flight of the wild goose, to the red maple leaf in fall, to corn shocks marching across a recently cut field.

- Love the earth, but respect it, too. It will constantly delight and surprise.

- Care for your soul by allowing your inner self to become exposed, as the soul of the earth is exposed each time a furrow is turned. When the earth is plowed, new life appears. When you allow your inner self the light of day, personal growth occurs.

- Spend lots of time outdoors. Dig in a garden, sit under a tree, fish in a pond, split wood, watch a deer.

- Watch the sunset each evening. It tells you about tomorrow's weather, but it also helps you celebrate the day's end with the promise of the sunrise.

- Take a grandchild for a walk in the woods. You'll both see more than either expected.

- It is both satisfying and terrifying to realize that nature can be more powerful than anything humans have invented.

- Walk quietly in the outdoors; if you are with someone, don't talk. You will see and hear so much more.

- When you hear the flocks of migrating Canada geese each spring and fall, look upward. See the grace and beauty, the cooperation and respect.

- Walk in a woods when it's ten below zero. Listen to the quiet of the frozen forest, and then be surprised by the occasional rifle-loud cracks of wood fiber exploding from the cold.

- Listen for the deathlike rattle of the dried oak leaves that hang on the trees in winter as a cold wind sweeps across the snow-covered woods.

- Develop a healthy respect for wasps, hornets, and bumblebees.

- Learn to value snakes. They have an important place.

- Develop respect for bats. They do not fly into your hair, but catch mosquitoes—thousands of them. Applaud the furry little creatures, and keep them working for you.

- If bats take up residence in an old farm building, leave them alone. During the daylight hours they sleep, coming out at night, so they will bother you little, except for some bat guano that may accumulate on the floor.

- Learn how to make a box trap. Trap a garden-raiding rabbit; haul it to a far corner of the

One with Nature

woods and release it. If it's fall, enjoy some rabbit stew.

- No matter how prepared we are, nature must be obeyed and always has the last word.

Nature's Beauty

- Although the beauty of nature may be all around us, we must take time to see it.

- Beauty is one of the many faces of nature.

- When you come upon a wild rose or a wild plum tree in bloom or a red or sweet clover plant, stop and marvel at the colors and how they change as the sun plays on the blossoms. Don't forget to put your nose to the blossoms and smell the subtle fragrances. Here is beauty at its finest.

- Hike to a high place in the country. Look out over the landscape, at the trees, at the planted fields, at the farmsteads, the sky, the birds, and the clouds.

- Walk to a high place on a clear night and look at the stars and the shadows, the blacks and the grays, and the immensity of the universe. Consider how insignificant each of us is, on this earth and beyond.

- Visit a pond on a snowy, windy day. Watch the wind paint pictures on the pond's surface as it creates swirls and ridges and then destroys them and creates something new, something completely different. Nature is an artist at work, but never satisfied with what it has created because it is always making something unique, something special.

- Stand under a big old tree on a sunny day in winter and look at the contrast of the bare, gray-brown branches with the clear blue sky.

- Watch a sandhill crane do its mating dance, a centuries-old choreography that is built into the DNA of this beautiful bird. A dance to impress a mate. A dance that is vigorous and exciting. And it works, too, because a pair of sandhill cranes have nested and raised young at the pond for many years.

- Pick up a white pinecone. Marvel at the intricacy of the design, of layers upon layers of woody material that have one purpose—protecting the tiny seeds that are tucked within the cone. Beauty is often associated with purpose—this is a good example.

- Watch a Karner blue butterfly work the lupine patch. The butterfly, no larger than your thumbnail, is blue with orange spots surrounding the wings, but you have to look closely. Something else to remember: beauty in nature is often found in the tiny creatures and in the tiny plants that are easily overlooked as we hurry along.

- Look for red hessian moss on the dry side of the hill that overlooks the prairie—it's a dry soil moss with little red fruiting bodies— named after the red uniforms of German Hessian soldiers, I'm told. A tiny little green plant with red accents.

- Gaze at a Baltimore oriole's nest, woven of dry grasses into a gourd-shaped structure that hangs from a tree branch and sways in the summer breeze. An engineering marvel.

- On a dewy morning, find a spiderweb and study it. It is the ultimate in engineering wisdom, with its thin threads of gossamer forming an intricate pattern with a center focal point where the spider often waits. For not only is the web a thing of beauty, but it is an intricate trap.

Weather

Rural people have long been interested in the weather. What they do each day and the day after that is affected by rain or sunshine, cold weather or warm, roaring winds or gentle breezes. It's the weather, largely, that determines a good year, an average year, or a terrible year for a farmer. Is it any wonder that rural folks are always trying to predict what kind of weather is on the way? Here are some weather predictors that have been passed down from generation to generation.

- Rain before seven, stop before eleven.

- Red sky at night, no rain in sight.

- Red sky in morning, time to take warning.

- If the dog is eating grass, rain within twenty-four hours.

- No dew in the morning, rain before night.

- April showers bring May flowers.

- Rain in May is a barn full of hay. Snow in May is a surprise.

- Rain in June is a silver spoon.
- The heavier a dog's hair in fall, the colder the winter.
- Little rainbows on each side of the sun (sun dogs) predict precipitation within forty-eight hours.
- A ring around the moon means a major change in the weather.
- A sliver of a new moon, tipped so you can't hang a pail of water on it, means rain within twenty-four hours.
- If among the clouds there is a patch of blue sky large enough to make a Dutchman's britches, clear weather is on the way.

Milkweed

I have several patches of milkweed on my farm, and although some consider them weeds, I have always been interested in the plant's qualities.

- Pull the leaf from a milkweed plant in summer and catch the milky ooze on your finger. What other plant has such interesting life juice?
- Notice how monarch butterflies are attracted to milkweed flowers; sometimes dozens of them congregate where milkweed grows in profusion. Learn about the special relationship between monarchs and milkweed. Monarchs lay their eggs on the underside of milkweed leaves, and when the eggs hatch, in a week or so, depending on the temperature, the larvae feed on the milkweed plant—the only thing they eat.
- Pick a milkweed pod in fall. Open it, allowing the hundreds of seeds, each attached to its own little parachute, to float free.
- Recall when you were in school and you painted empty milkweed pods with gold or silver paint and gave them to your mother as Christmas tree ornaments.
- Remember during World War II when you and your schoolmates collected milkweed pods for the war effort. They were used to make life vests.

Ponds

The pond on my farm offers more mystery and mystique than about anything else on my place. Something new is always happening there—including the rise and fall of the water level. In the forty-five years we've owned the farm, we've seen the pond increase and decrease in size twice—thus it appears to be on a twenty-year cycle. At its high point, the pond will cover five acres and be twenty feet deep in places. At its low point, it is about half an acre in size and only a few feet deep. We've seen beaver at the pond that succeeded in slicing off a goodly number of aspen trees, muskrats that have built elaborate cone-shaped houses, and ducks of various kinds that nest there, mostly teal, mallard, and wood. A pair of sandhill cranes regularly nests there, as does a pair of Canada geese. Songbirds of every stripe use the pond as a watering place, along with the deer, wild turkeys, raccoons, and an assortment of other critters. And the largest, meanest-looking snapping turtles live at the pond, unfortunately menacing the duck and gosling population.

There is much to be learned from sitting quietly by the pond, especially when the sun first peeks over the trees to the east, or the last light of evening sends the pond into deep shadows and the cooler temperature creates little fingers of fog that lift from the pond's surface.

- Sit quietly by a pond when the summer sun is sinking behind the trees and the birds are sharing their last quiet songs before day's end.

- Look for a doe and her fawn emerging out of the evening mists to drink at the pond's edge.

- Watch a mother raccoon teaching her little masked furry offspring how to fish from shore.

- Listen for the slap of a beaver's tail breaking the silence of the evening, letting you know that beavers are aware of your presence.

- Feel the early evening breeze sifting across the clearing and washing over the pond, riffling the surface.

- See little fingers of fog lifting from the water and hanging motionless, like translucent curtains hanging in front of nature's stage.

- Watch a mallard duck ease away from shore toward midpond, followed by six ducklings, one behind the other, the exact same distance apart. Swimming lessons.

- Sit on the shore of the pond on a warm afternoon in October. Watch the reflections in the water as the sun plays on the red maples, yellow aspens, and browning oak leaves.

- Drop a pebble into the water. Watch the splash and then the circles that form, ever larger, until they disappear—leaving the surface as smooth as before. When you are feeling overly important, think about the pebble, the splash, and the circles.

- Visit the pond on a warm spring evening, shortly after the ice melts. Listen to the frog song—these creatures celebrate the coming of spring with calls so loud that all other sounds are left in the background.

18

Place

Place can have special meaning. For those of us who grew up on farms, the home place was special, even though we may not have thought it so at the time. Today, many years later, we remember every room in the old farmhouse and what went on in them. We remember fondly the big kitchen, with its wood-burning cookstove that produced loaf after loaf of homemade bread, sweet rolls, and pies. We remember the smells of the cooking as well as the tastes. We remember the dining room, with its round oak heater that kept us warm in winter, when most of the house was closed off. One bedroom, where we slept, was heated partially from the stovepipe that stuck up through the floor and then pushed into the brick chimney. The room, not as cold certainly from the other two upstairs bedrooms, was far from comfortable on below-zero nights.

The cow barn, two stories with hayloft above and cow stable below, was where we spent much of our time—milking cows, tossing down silage, forking hay from the haymow, feeding calves, and several other daily barn chores.

And, of course, the farm fields, the hilly, stony fields, each one with a story or two or three to tell as we grew corn and oats, alfalfa and potatoes on these rough, sandy acres. The twenty-acre woodlot north of the house is filled with memories, of cutting wood for the woodstove, of hunting squirrels and rabbits for the supper table, or of just walking and listening and not doing much of anything.

But there are more than memories, more

than stories to recall of the home place where you learned to work, do chores on time, respect animals, get along with your siblings, and obey your parents. The home place left an indelible imprint on each of us, and for those of us who left the home place to seek our fortunes elsewhere, more than we realized at the time. I was one of those who didn't want people to know that I grew up without electricity, never knew indoor plumbing while at home, and was warmed with a wood-burning stove. It took me awhile to realize that the influence of the home place on who I am could not be denied, as hard as I, at one time, tried to deny it. The home place is my history, and I have since learned that we are our histories, whether we like it or not.

Those who were born and raised on farms and then spent their entire lives on the home place often find it necessary to leave when they become older. Leaving the home place is never easy—especially when one is older. Too many stories and too many memories to leave behind.

For all of us, where we grew up has shaped our beliefs and values—has influenced our decisions about what is important and less important in our lives. Those of us who grew up on farms have a special way of looking at the world; our views are neither better nor worse than those without farm experience, but they are often different. The home place has had a great influence on our lives.

Home

- Home is where you can go when no one else will take you in.

- As much as we think we've left home, we really never have.

- The home place will be forever in our hearts.

- Can't wait to return.

- Home is where you can say anything, because nobody listens to you anyway.

- When you are home, you are most like what you really are.

- When you are home, you can scratch where it itches.

- There's no place like home.

- As hard as we may try to deny the influence of the home place, we cannot. It is forever a part of who we are, whether we realize it or not.

- Love begins at home.

- When there is no place else to go, there is always home.

- Our feet may leave home, but never our hearts.

- For a person, home is where everything begins.

- What a child learns at home they will remember forever.

- Even chickens come home to roost.

- A home is but a house without people within it.

Sacred Places

Sacred places are special places—most of us have them. For some people they are the home place, but for others sacred places exist elsewhere. I have two such places that I return to regularly. One of them is the Boundary Waters Canoe Area Wilderness, in Northern Minnesota. For more than twenty-five years, one or more members of my family and I have returned there every year for rest and renewal. The BWCAW is one of the few places left in the world where there is no light pollution or no background traffic noise; cell phones don't work there, and the nearest drive-in is more than fifty miles away. I need some time each year in a wilderness area where the loon calls in the night and a gentle breeze sends waves lapping on the stones beneath my campsite.

My sixty-acre farm in central Wisconsin, which my family and I have owned since 1966, is my second sacred place. I return there often to dig in my garden, split wood for the stoves that heat the place, and hike the trails that thread through the pine plantations we have planted over the years and are now of various sizes. Here is where I find solitude. Here is where I watch the seasons change. Here is where I observe the wildlife that lives at my place—wild turkeys, deer, cottontail rabbits, ruffed grouse, and many more creatures. Here is where I watch my prairie restoration project that has slowly moved from cornfield to what it was when the land was first plowed, in 1867. It is here that I discover deeper meanings, about nature and about me. I have learned much from this place. There is much more to learn. Wisdom abounds on these sandy acres.

- We all need places of wonder and joy to return to.
- A sacred place is where we can find solitude and renewal.
- Loving a place is as natural as loving a person.
- It is great fun to explore a place that does not appear on any map.
- Sometimes it seems that the only places left to explore are the deeper recesses of our minds.
- When exploring a scared place, any place for that matter, look for the little things, the overlooked things—a remnant of barbed wire growing out of a tree (once a boundary marker), a mound of soil a hundred rods long (what a sandstorm did to the land back in the dry years of the 1930s).
- Know the power of place.

19

Remembering

Remembering earlier days is more than nostalgia. Remembering helps people recall their roots and their values. Many rural people live on land that was settled by ancestors three or four generations ago. A grandfather may have built the barn at the turn of the century. A great-grandfather probably cleared the twenty-acre field to the north when he first arrived from Germany.

Reminders of the past are all around, helping us remember others that have gone this way before—plowed the fields, harvested the grain, milked the cows, fed the pigs, attended church, sent children to the one-room country school, celebrated holidays, and did many of the things that rural people do today.

Sometimes it is fun to take time out, sit quietly, and reflect on our memories. Here are some of my memories, which may evoke memories for you:

- I remember, as a child, how important and special was a new pair of shoes, and how wonderful, too, was a new pair of bib overalls, with their blue denim smell and freshness. How I resisted their washing, for in the washing some of their specialness was lost.

- I remember my first day of school in first grade, when I was five years old and the smallest, youngest kid in our one-room country school. I sat quietly at my desk, the smell of freshly oiled floors engulfing me and the idea of spending eight years here overwhelming me.

- I remember the country mill that was powered by water, how the building shuddered and shook when the grinding began, how we dumped cob corn into the maw of the

Rural Wit and Wisdom

mill, and how fluffy, sweet-smelling cow feed emerged a few minutes later.

- I remember the miller having a fish line dangling in the millpond, hoping to hook one of the giant trout that everyone knew lived there but no one had ever seen, and how sweet the water tasted from the pipe that was tapped into a free-flowing spring near the mill dam.

- I remember the county fair, with its Ferris wheel and merry-go-round and the aroma of fried onions mixing with animal smells from the cattle barns. I recall the yell of the carnival hawkers, "Three balls for a quarter!" "Ring the post and win a stuffed animal!" "Knock over the milk bottles and take home a genuine Indian relic!" (made in Japan).

- I remember how proud I felt when my 4-H calf won a blue ribbon and how proud, too, was my father, who helped me lead my little Holstein bull calf back to the cattle barn from the show ring.

- I remember harness horses—pacers and trotters that pulled little buggies with bicycle tires around the dusty racetrack. I recall the time when something frightened one of the horses and it reared up, slipped, and sat down on the buggy, blowing out both of the tires and ending the race for the driver that day.

- I remember the bright red, two-winged, two-seater, open-cockpit airplane that gave half-hour rides for fifty cents. The pilot took off and landed from an improvised landing strip in a pasture back of the fairground's horse barn. I watched the plane, with its first customer aboard, bump along the rough landing strip, its engine roaring. It slowly lifted into the air, not a minute too soon in order to climb over the row of oak trees that bordered the pasture.

- I remember gravel country roads twisting through the countryside, along the streams, through the valleys, around steep hills, and sometimes straight as a tight string when the country was flat.

- I recall country roads in winter, with wind-blown snow sifting over the tops of snow-drifts, making the roads impassable as the snow accumulated.

- I remember spring mud and how the milkman—destined to travel the roads in all kinds of weather—sometimes needed the assistance of our team of horses, or tractor, to pull him from the quagmire that was the road in front of our farm.

- I remember clouds of summer dust announcing a traveler on the road, maybe a salesman coming to our farm, especially if the dust cloud appeared in the afternoon.

- I remember my mother's disdain for dust in any form, on any day, for it sifted into the house and gathered on the top of the dining room table and, less noticeably, on the clock shelf, along the tops of the pictures, and just about everywhere.

- I remember Christmas morning, with a stack of presents under the tree that could not be opened until the morning milking was done. I recall receiving new socks and mittens that grandmother had knitted, and a new pair of skates, the type that clamped onto the bottom of my shoes and were tightened with a key.

- I remember walking a mile to the neighbor's with a small present and a freshly baked pie, because we knew that his wife had passed away and his children had grown and moved to the city, and he was there alone on Christmas Day.

- I remember Christmas dinner, with aunts and uncles and cousins, and a table spread with food like I only saw when the threshing crews came.

- I remember the smell and taste of fresh-made bread, spread thick with butter and home-made strawberry jam.

- I remember the Sears and Roebuck catalog that came each spring and fall, creating never-ending wishes and eventually ending up in the little house back of the big house.

- I remember the country mailman, who made the rounds each day, Monday through Saturday, no matter what the weather. I watched for the cloud of dust on our country road at eleven each day, because that was the time he came.

- I remember the party line telephone, with ten customers, each with a special ring, long and three shorts, three shorts, and so on. When the phone rang, you picked up the receiver whether it was your ring or not. It was how you kept track of the news in the community, both good and bad, exciting and ordinary.

- I remember Fanny, our farm dog, who ruled over the area between the house and the barn—the dooryard, farm people called this space. Fanny announced the arrival of all cars to the dooryard. City salesmen often misunderstood the dog's intentions and sometimes stayed in their cars, tooting their horns, hoping my mother would come outside. Usually she didn't. She figured if a salesman couldn't face a friendly farm dog, he wasn't much of a salesman. After a brief period of horn tooting and waiting, he usually left.

- I remember how Fanny kept the chickens in the chicken yard, the area immediately around the chicken house, barking at them if they strayed, or even rolling them in the dust if she thought they needed a stronger lesson.

- I remember Fanny keeping track of my little twin brothers playing in the sand hole by the barn, nudging them back if they decided to stray toward the road.

20

Storytelling

Storytelling is as old as civilization, going back to the days when cave dwellers gathered in front of a smoky fire to recount the details of the day's hunt or recall tales of earlier hunts and happenings in the past. Storytelling is a human activity; it ties people together, and it can help bridge the generations when grandparents share with grandkids their stories of years ago. Storytelling is also a way of recording and sharing history. And for the storyteller, sharing events from one's life can help make sense out of the teller's life.

The rural heartland has many storytellers. I grew up hearing the stories of my parents, my aunts and uncles, and my grandparents. These were my first, and in many ways my fondest, memories of growing up. When our extended family gathered to celebrate birthdays, Thanksgiving, Christmas, and Easter, there were always the stories, generally prompted by some youngster who would ask, "What happened back when you were a kid and that big storm blew in out of the west?" The tale would begin, and everyone listened attentively, even though they may have heard the story dozens of times before. With each telling, something new emerged, some added nuance, some additional description, a new piece of dialogue. And thus the story provided new meaning, as well as entertainment.

As country folk gathered for such community events as barn raisings, grain threshing, country school programs, and church picnics, storytelling always emerged as a major activity.

Rural people like to tell stories; they also like to hear and read them. With the coming of television, computers, and advanced technology, storytelling has waned. It has drifted into the shadows of history. Yet stories and storytelling remain important, and there appears to be a renewed interest in this art form. One of the reasons why, I believe, is that stories are the essence of our humanity.

Stories may be shared orally, written, or both spoken and written. I do both. I firmly believe that all stories should be written so they can become a permanent part of the historical record for a family and for a community. These stories should be shared with family members, and, as importantly, they should be filed with the local historical society and the public library. Some story wisdom:

- Stories are a way of recalling the past while opening a window to the future.
- People hunger for a good story.
- Stories are the history of a civilization.
- The best way to learn, and often the easiest, is with a story.
- In the midst of controversy and disagreement, a good story can often bring a smile to everyone and thus calm down a contentious situation.
- Stories may be sad, hilarious, truthful, or heavily embellished. It doesn't matter. What matters is the story.
- The pictures in the stories we tell are many times better than those on television or in movies.
- Old farm buildings have stories to tell, stories about who built them, how they were used, what happened inside of them as the years passed. It takes a bit more work to dig out an old building's story, but the story is there. Go looking—and listening.
- The land is an ever-changing story that begs to be told.
- We think with words and pictures; we learn through stories.
- A story gives people an opportunity to think for themselves.

Rural Wit and Wisdom

- A story can be about almost anything. Sometimes the simplest ideas are the most profound.

- A good story evokes emotion, a driving force in our lives.

- Stories are where a society's values are found.

- Facts tell us about an event; stories evoke our feelings and deeper thoughts.

- Storytelling is an art form, as important as music, painting, sculpture, and other art forms.

- Through our stories we can express our creativity.

- When we forget our stories, we forget who we are.

Storytellers

- The history of a community resides in its storytellers.

- Every person has a story to tell, no matter what age, no matter what background, no matter where the person lives or has lived.

- As we share our stories, we share some of who we are.

- Stories may be told aloud and in person, written on a piece of paper and shared, or recorded on some fancy new recording device—what matters is that the story is shared and saved.

- Unfortunately, television and movies have become the present-day storytellers.

- Storytelling can take us to a place within ourselves where we have never been. It can change us forever.

- Storytelling can help us come out from behind ourselves.

- Through storytelling, we can discover meaning without defining it.

- A story not told is a piece of history lost.

Writing Your Story

I have taught Writing from Your Life workshops for more than forty years, helping people of all ages reconnect to their memories and write down their stories. For those who have not done this, the two biggest questions or concerns I hear are "I don't remember much about my life" and "What should I write about?"

Many of my students have the mistaken idea that they should try to write the entire story of their life, from their first memory to the present time. When they consider this, most of them are immediately overwhelmed. There is just so much, even though, ironically, many of them say they don't remember much about it.

I suggest the following as a more manageable way of writing about your life. Write about:

- Growing-up years, from first memories through high school years.

- A special time in your life (military, work years, etc.).

- A special place in your life. Almost everyone has a special place they like to visit; some refer to these places as sacred, places with a special meaning to which they return again and again.

- Special events in your life (joyous or sad): Marriage. Divorce. Birth of a child.

- A special person (people) in your life. This may be one or both of your parents, a favorite teacher, a religious leader, a mentor, or a friend who has made a difference in your life.

- Turning points in your life: A promotion. Loss of a job. Serious illness.

- Special things you remember: A birthday party. When you first saw an ocean. A special friend from elementary school. Your first love.

For recalling memories, I have developed a series of prompts—questions to ask yourself that help push aside the cobwebs in your memory and reveal the stories that are there and itching to be told.

Early Years (Up to Age 12)

- Describe your school in detail, including the floor plan. What are your favorite memories of when you were an elementary school student? What story do you remember most vividly about elementary school?

- What was your greatest fear when you were a child? Can you recall something that happened when you were especially afraid? Who or what was involved?

- What games did you play at school and at home? Any stories associated with these games?

- Do you remember when you learned to ride a bike? What were the circumstances?

- What was your favorite toy? Your favorite book when you were a child?

- Describe Christmas or some other holiday important to your family. Recall a story when you were particularly happy, or one when you were particularly sad.

- Do you recall any trips you made with your family?

- What was your greatest achievement in high school?

- How did you learn to drive a car? What happened? Who taught you?

- What happened when you went for your driver's license?

- Describe your first love.

- Who were your idols? Your heroes?

- Did you participate in sports? Which ones?

- Describe your first job for pay. How much did you earn?

- What was your favorite music? Your favorite books?

Teen Years (13–19)

- What rules did your family have for you? Recall a story of when you broke these rules.

- Describe school. What story or stories describe your good times in high school? The bad times?

- Who were your best friends? How would you describe them?

Young Adult Years (19–25)

- Did you have schooling after high school? Post–high school education stories?

- Did you serve in the military?

- What was your first full-time job? What was the pay? Describe the job.

- Who were your best friends?

- Where did you live, and what was it like?
- What were your favorite books and music?
- How did you meet your spouse?

Early Marriage Years (20–30)

- Describe your marriage ceremony. Anything go wrong?
- Did you take a honeymoon? Do you have memories or stories from that time?
- Where did you live? What stories do you have of your first year together? What was memorable? Are there things you would like to forget, but your spouse won't let you?
- When did you have children? What stories are associated with the birth of your first child? Your later children?
- What rules did you establish at home?
- If you did not marry during this time, describe your life during these years.
- What leisure-time activities did you pursue?

Early Career (20–35)

- What accomplishments are you most proud of?
- What are the toughest problems you faced? Pick one and write a story about it.
- Did you have any major problems in your home during this time?
- What is the most important thing that happened to you during this time?
- Did you change jobs or careers?
- Were you ever laid off from work?
- What was your relationship with your children like during these years?
- What continuing education did you participate in?

Middle Years (35–65)

- Describe your relationship with your parents.
- What were your feelings when your children left home?
- Describe your relationship with your brothers and sisters.

- What were your hobbies? How have they changed over the years?
- Did you participate in volunteer activities?
- What were the critical events that marked this period in your life?

Later Years (65 and Beyond)

- What stories do you have about retirement? And what feelings did you have at the time?
- Where have you traveled? Are there places you want to return to? Places you never want to see again? What places are you looking forward to discovering?
- What health challenges have you faced?
- What are your proudest achievements?
- What volunteer activities do you participate in?

The following are additional ways to wake up your memories, to help you recall the details of your life that may be a bit cloudy and difficult to pin down.

- Visit a museum or a historic site with exhibits representing the years you are writing about.
- Listen to music of the time in which you are interested.
- Look at old photos.
- Sit down with siblings, other relatives, or old friends and swap stories of the time you are interested in.
- Page through an old Sears, Roebuck and Co. or Montgomery Ward catalog.
- Review old newspapers of the day (available at many historical societies).
- Visit antique stores.
- Return to the place where you grew up.

Yet another way to recall your memories is to do these exercises:

- Draw the floor plan for the house you lived in when you were ten to twelve years old. Put the furniture in the rooms, place the pictures on the walls, and indicate the family members associated with each room. Jot down the smells associated with each room. Mention your feelings associated with various rooms. When finished drawing, write a story about something that happened in one of the rooms.

• Draw a straight line on a big sheet of paper. Along the line, indicate the turning points in your life (graduation, marriage, divorce, birth of a child, serious illness, death of a loved one, etc.). Select one of the turning points and write a story about it.

• Mind mapping is another way to recall memories. Here is how you do it:

1. Draw a circle in the middle of a blank sheet of paper.

2. Write the idea you want to focus on in that circle. For instance, if you want to recall something about your first job for pay, write "First job for pay" (or the actual job title) in the circle. If you want to discover memories about your mother, write "Mom" in the circle, and so on.

3. Focus on the circle. Think of everything associated with the topic you have written there.

4. As you recall something, draw a line from the center circle, make another circle at the end of the line, and write this recollection in it. As you think of ideas related to the most recent circle, write them and draw further circles around them. Soon you will have many circles around the larger circle in the center.

5. Do this for ten to fifteen minutes. You'll surprise yourself as to how many events and stories you'll remember and how much specific information you can recall. Each new circle will likely trigger yet additional ideas.

• In addition to recalling memories, mind mapping can also be used to organize your writing. For instance, if you are mind mapping the topic "First job for pay," the first group of circles might include such information as, "Where I worked," "How much I was paid," "Relationship with my boss," "What I learned from this job," and so on. These circles can be organizers for your story—perhaps subheads for sections, or the beginnings for paragraphs.

Rural Wit and Wisdom

Writing Tips

- Be yourself. Write the way you talk.

- Put in dates and places. When discussing some process, include the steps. "To make wine, first we found some wild grapes, then we…"

- Be sure to include the time the story took place.

- Include details: color, size, and smells. Tell your story in such a way that your reader can see himself or herself in this situation, in this place, at the particular time you are writing about. Details make the difference.

- Write about ordinary things: Your first ice cream cone. A book you fondly remember. A place you enjoyed visiting.

- Use dialogue.

- Be honest. Write about things as they happened, not as you wished they had happened. Some things you may wish to leave out, but be honest about what you include.

- Only *you* can avoid a family feud over skeletons you unearth or don't.

- When possible, write about your life as a story—after all, it is a story.

Guidelines for Story Writing

- A story has a beginning, a middle, and an end and generally should be written in that order. Some would-be storytellers begin their story with the punch line. Not a good idea. Why bother to read the rest of the story if you know how it will end?

- A story includes characters, which usually are people, but may be animals, the weather, or an inanimate object such as a tree or a pond, a barn or the farm tractor. Human characters are brought to life through physical description, names, dialogue, how they use words, their actions and mannerisms.

- Most stories have a conflict: between people, between a person and an animal, between a person and the weather, etc.

- A story shows rather than tells. Showing encourages readers or listeners to develop their own meaning through the storyteller's use of description, suspense, detail, dialogue, and sense of place. For example, rather than writing, "Joe was a decidedly homely man," you might write, "Joe had a red bulbous nose, ears that resembled an elephant's, and a chin that looked like someone had hit him in the face with a shovel."

- A storyteller should evoke as many senses as possible in telling the story: hearing, sight, touch, smell, and taste.

- Stories may be humorous or sad but in all instances should evoke emotion.

- Stories are generally written at more than one level. Stories should be interesting and entertaining. At a deeper level, they may inform or teach, and at the deepest level may evoke some change in the reader or the listener's way of thinking.

The Creative Self and the Judging Self

Trying to write everything perfectly the first time blocks many writers. They fuss over whether words are spelled correctly, whether the commas are in the right place, and whether everything makes sense. As a result, they accomplish little as they write and rewrite their first paragraphs or sometimes even their first sentences.

We each have within us a creative self and a judging self. For most of us, the judging self is better developed—it's the part of us that looks over our shoulder at everything we do and makes some comment about it. This is especially true in writing when the judging self examines every word we write and usually has something negative to say about it. Here's one solution to the problem: When you begin writing a story from your life, keep going. Don't stop to correct things, but forge on. Later, you can come back and make the necessary corrections. By doing this, you are allowing your creative self to take over, to ply your memory and sift out the stories that reside there—and put them down on paper.

If you have difficulty going on because the judging self is always there making nasty comments about your work, try this: Select a topic you want to write about, perhaps a story about your favorite toy when you were a child or a story about something someone did for you

that made a difference in your life. Set your kitchen timer for ten minutes, and write non-stop until the bell rings. This is called forced writing. The technique allows your creative self to come into its own and at the same time frustrates the judging self, because by the time it wants to tell you to change something, you are already onto something else. I've used forced writing with my writing students many times over the years. It works for most people, but not all. You'll have to decide if it works for you.

Revising and Rewriting

Many professional writers spend more time revising and rewriting than they do creating the first draft. That is certainly the case for me. I spend up to three times as much time, sometimes more, polishing my writing as I do creating the first version of it. Here are some of the steps I follow in the process of revising and rewriting my material.

1. Write a piece all the way through before beginning to revise it.

2. Set it aside for a month or so, and work on something else.

3. After the piece has rested, read it all the way through without stopping. Then ask, What is this piece about? Write the answer to the question in a sentence or two. The answer is the theme of the piece.

4. Read the piece again, referring often to the theme. Remove everything that doesn't contribute to the theme. Note where the information contributing to the theme may be a bit thin and may require additional research and writing.

5. Read the piece once more, looking for the logic of what you have written. Does the piece need some reorganization to make understanding it more clear?

6. Read the first paragraph to make sure it will grab the reader's attention.

7. Read the entire piece aloud or, even better, read it into a voice recorder and then listen to it. Listen for rough spots

and the rhythm of the writing, and make corrections as necessary.

8. Check for grammatical errors and spelling mistakes.

9. Have at least one other person, usually not your spouse, read the piece and give you an honest appraisal of the writing.

Journaling

For most people, the more they write, the easier it becomes. One way to stay in practice is to keep a journal. In it, record the weather. Write down the activities of the day, the good and the bad, the joys and the disappointments, and your feelings toward all. As you write, a great load will often lift from your shoulders. You'll also have a record that you can go back to to see what your life was like at an earlier age. Here are some further benefits from journaling:

- The process of writing helps to clarify thoughts, feelings, and observations.

- Writing the words creates a historical record of more permanence than thoughts, which are often fleeting.

- Journaling forces the writer to consider what in life is most important. People simply do not have time to record everything, thus they are forced to make value judgments about their experiences.

- Journaling can often help people define problems they are having in their lives—and in many instances can help to resolve the problems.

- Journaling is a creative process. As people write, they discover thoughts and ideas they didn't know they possessed.

- Journals are excellent places for venting frustrations about people and events, allowing pent-up emotions to have an opportunity for expression.

- Drawings and sketches can be incorporated into journals as a way of adding a visual dimension to thoughts and feelings.

Six-Word Story

An interesting exercise is to write about something that happened in your life in six words. By doing so, you make every word count. It's a way of getting to the nub of your story without beating around the bush with extra and sometimes distracting material. Ernest Hemingway is credited with a six-word story that went as follows: "For Sale: Baby shoes, never worn." As a child I had polio. One of my six-word stories is: "Polio at twelve. Still limping today."

Some life-story writers may begin with a six-word story and then expand it into a much longer story—the six-word story helps to keep them focused as they develop the more complex and complete story.

Afterword

Increasing numbers of people these days are interested in the wit and wisdom from the heartland. This has not always been so. In the late 1970s and early 1980s, I worked part-time as an acquisitions editor for the McGraw-Hill Book Company in New York. My boss at McGraw-Hill, someone who had grown up in the East and spent his entire life there, had little knowledge of or respect for the heartland. In his mind, this piece of geography that I call home was a vast wasteland, a part of the country to pass through or over quickly on the way to the West Coast, where important things happened along with the even more important things occurring on the East Coast. All of this is changing. We who live in the heartland have long known that important things happen here, and underneath what goes on here is a foundation of beliefs and values that have lasting benefits. We heartland people are modest, perhaps too modest at times. We know what we believe, what we value, but we don't brag about it, don't run around shouting, "Look here! Look at us! Look what's going on out in in the middle of the country." It's just not our way. So it has taken awhile for the two coasts and the major urban areas in the country to discover us and to realize that what goes on out here in the small towns and farms, in the hinterlands, may be of value to others, beyond those of us who live here in the heartland of the country.

Jerry Apps writes novels and nonfiction about the outdoors, country life, and rural living. He received the 2008 First Place Nature Writing Award from the Midwest Independent Publishers Association and the 2007 Major Achievement Award from the Council for Wisconsin Writers. He and his wife live in Madison, Wisconsin.

Steve Apps is an award-winning photojournalist with twenty-five years in the newspaper industry. As chief photographer for the *Wisconsin State Journal*, he has covered a wide range of assignments, including the Green Bay Packers and the University of Wisconsin–Madison sports.